'Nelson's account is lucid, her h[...]
strong. Memories of her childhood [...]
who died when she was a girl – [...]
charged elements. But her wry a[...]
clownish calamity of the courtr[...]
media circus (Nelson was on 48[...]
affecting . . . A much-needed [...]
painful aftermath of [...]
Booklis[...]

'*The Red Parts* feels rushed, frenzi[...]
way. While the reopening of Ja[...]
the book is also an autopsy, an exa[...]
explicit) on our cultural fascination [...]
and misogyny. Instead of distancing [...]
Nelson is fascinated by them, and a [...]
her inability to escape from certain [...]
these be "murder mind," "suicide [...]
(though no less traumatic) ruts – [...]
junkie boyfriend, abandonment by [...]
her mother and extended family [...]
the trial. In sum, *The Red P[...]*
Pop Matt[...]

'A bool[...]
A genre-buster w[...]

[...]subject
[...]he [...]t ever[...]
N[...]n refuse[...] service brands, including Glasgow
unknown. A necessa[...]w.glasgowlife.org.uk) are operating
[...]port Glasgow

' Every bit as gripping a[...]
more complex an[...]
Vultu[...]

is as magnetic as Joan Didion bu[...] style, Nelson intertwine[...], and true-crime tidbits into a[...] Nelson eschews tidy resolution[...] re imperfect – and yet she also[...] ome totally worthwhile'
[...]ut

[...] between a narrative of [...] her own life, Nelson examine[...]

[...] son has made her own box [...] things. It's not a beautiful [...] shimmering one, which [...] t that can affect a family [...] r a violent loss'
[...] Chronicle

[...] ead – Didion-esque in its [...] nt, and its sheen. Like any [...] is a born trespasser, with an [...] science. From nightmare she [...] elible literature'
[...] thor of *Humiliation*

[...] along that combines such [...] precision with the sense [...] life. *The Red Parts* is on[...] ing, genre-defying acco[...] nd pushes further into[...] nd deeply brave achie[...] llard

[...]-crime book, but i[...] d rewarding'
[...]e.

MAGGIE NELSON

The Red Parts

Autobiography of a Trial

VINTAGE

3 5 7 9 10 8 6 4 2

Vintage
20 Vauxhall Bridge Road,
London SW1V 2SA

Vintage is part of the Penguin Random House group of companies
whose addresses can be found at global.penguinrandomhouse.com.

Copyright © Maggie Nelson 2007
Preface © Maggie Nelson 2015

Maggie Nelson has asserted her right to be identified as the
author of this Work in accordance with the Copyright,
Designs and Patents Act 1988

Published by Vintage in 2017
First published by Free Press, a division of Simon & Schuster, Inc. in 2007

penguin.co.uk/vintage

A CIP catalogue record for this book is available from the British Library

ISBN 9781784705794

Printed and bound by Clays Ltd, Elcograf S.p.A

Penguin Random House is committed to a sustainable future
for our business, our readers and our planet. This book is made
from Forest Stewardship Council® certified paper.

For Christina Crosby and Janet Jakobsen,
who train in the fire, and do the world justice.

For there is nothing covered, that shall not be revealed; neither hid, that shall not be known.

—LUKE 12:2

In all desire to know there is already a drop of cruelty.

—NIETZSCHE

Contents

Preface   xvii

Murder Mind   1

An Inheritance   11

The Face of Evil   19

A Live Stream   25

The Red Parts   33

Addendum   43

Red House   51

American Taboo   65

Murder Mind, Redux   75

To Hell or Bust   81

Sybaris   93

After Justice   107

The Book of Shells   117

At the Tracks   127

Gary   133

Contents

Poetic License   145

The End of the Story   151

In the Victim Room   161

Primetime   171

Open Murder   177

The Hand of God   181

Coda   193

Sources and Resources   197

Acknowledgments   201

Preface

At the opening of Peter Handke's *A Sorrow Beyond Dreams*, a devastating sliver of a book that Handke reportedly wrote in the two months directly following his mother's suicide, he writes: "My mother has been dead for almost seven weeks; I had better get to work before the need to write about her, which I felt so strongly at her funeral, dies away and I fall back into the dull speechlessness with which I reacted to the news of her suicide. Yes, get to work. . . . As usual when engaged in literary work, I am alienated from myself and transformed into an object, a remembering and formulating machine."

The reopening of my aunt Jane's murder case in 2005— though nowhere near as psychically catastrophic as a mother's suicide—induced in me a remarkably similar mood. After attending the suspect's trial in July 2005, I felt an intense rush to record all the details before being swallowed up, be it by anxiety, grief, amnesia, or horror; to transform myself or my material into an aesthetic object, one which might stand next to, or in for, or as the last impediment to, the dull speechlessness that makes remembering and formulating impossible. And so. After the trial, *nel mezzo del camin,* I set up shop in a city completely alien to me

(Los Angeles), and wrote this account in a heightened, concentrated, occasionally reckless state of mind. *A Sorrow Beyond Dreams* sat on my desk throughout, as goad and guide. *Yes, get to work.*

What effect do years, even decades, have on a piece of writing that self-consciously attests to the turbulent, raw, and rushed circumstances of its composition and publication? In the case of Handke's book, the performance feels no less electric, but time has added to it a certain uncanniness—that of psychological exigency suspended eerily, beautifully, in that outside-of-time place that literature can create. I can only hope something of the same might be said of this new edition of *The Red Parts,* which has given me the dual gift of protecting the book (for the time being, anyway) from a different kind of dull speechlessness—that of unavailability—while also bringing into focus the book I always hoped *The Red Parts* might one day become: a peculiar, pressurized meditation on time's relation to violence, to grief, thankfully untethered from the garish rubrics of "current events," "true crime," or even "memoir."

One aim I had while writing was to allow the events of the trial, the events of my childhood, the events of Jane's murder, and the act of writing to share a single spatial and temporal moment. At one point in *The Red Parts,* this intermingling is imagined as a place, a "dark crescent of land, where suffering is essentially meaningless, where the present collapses into the past without warning, where we cannot escape the fates we fear the most, where heavy rains come and wash bodies up and out of their graves, where grief lasts forever and its force never fades." I'm glad to say that the prescriptive severity of this image has receded for me, at least for the moment. But the importance of allowing oneself (of allowing myself, I should say) to stay in its grip for some real time has not. I'm grateful, once again, to send in this report from the field.

Maggie Nelson
Los Angeles, 2015

The Red Parts

Murder Mind

*W*E HAVE EVERY *reason to believe this case is moving swiftly toward a successful conclusion.*

These were the words spoken by a detective from the Michigan State Police, in a phone call to my mother, one afternoon in early November 2004. After hanging up with the detective, my mother called me and repeated the message.

His words stunned me. As she said them I watched the hallway of my apartment tilt slightly downward, as if momentarily flirting with the idea of becoming a funhouse.

His words had stunned her also. She received his call on her cell phone while driving, and immediately had to pull over to the side of the dusty road near her home in northern California to absorb their impact.

The case in question was that of the 1969 murder of her younger sister, Jane Mixer, which had gone officially unsolved for the past thirty-five years. The detective said he had been working on it feverishly for the past five, but hadn't wanted to call until an arrest was imminent. Which it now was.

This news would have been shocking in and of itself, but its timing made it uncanny.

For the past five years, I had also been working feverishly on my aunt's case, albeit from a different angle. I had been researching and writing a poetry book about her life and death titled *Jane: A Murder,* which was just about to be published. I had no idea that Jane's case had been active; my book was about a cold case abandoned by investigators long ago. It was about how one might live—or, rather, how my family lived, how I lived—under the shadow of the death of a family member who had clearly died horribly and fearfully, but under circumstances that would always remain unknown, unknowable.

When I first meet this detective—Detective-Sergeant Eric Schroeder—at a preliminary hearing for the suspect, Gary Earl Leiterman, on January 14, 2005—he will greet me with a bear hug, saying, *I bet you thought you were working on this alone all these years.*

Indeed, I had.

I GREW UP knowing that my mother had a younger sister named Jane who had been murdered, but that was about all I knew. I knew Jane had been twenty-three when she died, and in her first year of law school at the University of Michigan. I knew my mother was twenty-five at the time, and recently married to my father. Neither my sister Emily nor I had yet been born. We were born in northern California, where our parents moved in the wake of Jane's death—Emily in 1971, me in 1973.

I had the vague sense while growing up that the deaths

of other girls were somehow related to Jane's murder, but I didn't know how. Then one afternoon, home alone, around thirteen, looking for a book in my mother's office, I spotted the spine of a book I'd never noticed before. Though nearly out of sight and reach, the garish, tabloid lettering, which read *The Michigan Murders*, stood out among the highbrow literary classics that my mother read and taught. I got up on a chair to pull the squat paperback down.

This simple act carried its own legacy of trepidation, as the first of the many bones I broke as a child—in this case, a cracked elbow that occasioned reconstructive surgery and weeks spent motionless in traction—was the result of climbing a bookshelf in pursuit of a book. That accident had happened in a bookstore in Sausalito, the harbor town outside of San Francisco where I lived for the first few years of my life. I was only two at the time, but I remember a brightly colored rabbit on the book's cover, and I remember wanting it desperately.

After this accident I began to have a recurring dream. It was a dream of falling—or jumping—off the carport of our house in Sausalito onto the driveway, and hence to my death. I must have been dreaming this dream very young, threeish. In the dream a crowd of people come to look at my body, which lies at the bottom of the driveway as if at the base of a steep Greek amphitheater. It is difficult to remember the tone of the dream now: I remember horror at my action, a sense of detachment, a deep sadness, and some discomfort in watching my body be scrutinized as a corpse.

The cover of *The Michigan Murders* depicted a faux-photograph of a Farrah Fawcett–like model, half of her face peeling away to reveal an infrared negative. Its coloring and graphics, along with the furtiveness I felt in examining it, immediately brought to mind a certain issue of *Playboy* I had spent a great deal of time studying as a child in my father's bathroom—the Valentine's Day issue from 1980, featuring Suzanne Somers. I remember that my father had liked Suzanne Somers very much.

I opened to the first page of *The Michigan Murders* and read: *In a two-year period, seven young women were murdered in Washtenaw County, some in so brutal a fashion as to make the Boston Strangler look like a mercy killer.*

I flipped through the book anxiously, hungry to find something, anything, about Jane, about my family. I quickly gathered that all the names had been changed. But I suspected I was getting close when I read:

A trooper had brought the 1968 University of Michigan Yearbook [to the crime scene], and the smiling likeness in it of graduating senior Jeanne Lisa Holder of Muskegon, Michigan, did bear a resemblance to the puffed face of the young woman stretched out lifeless in Pleasantview Cemetery.

"Jeanne Lisa Holder" bore a resemblance to "Jane Louise Mixer." One layer had begun to peel.

• • •

Murder Mind

YEARS LATER, while in the thick of researching and writing *Jane*, the problem was not too little information. It was too much. Not about Jane—her murder remained maddeningly opaque—but about the other girls, whose horrific rapes and murders were described in excruciating detail in newspapers from the period, several true crime books, and on many "serial killer chic" Web sites. There were charts such as the one that appeared in the *Detroit Free Press* on July 28, 1969, titled "A Pattern of Death: An Anatomy of 7 Brutal Murders," which organized the details under the categories "Last Seen," "Where Found," "How Killed," "Other Injuries," etc. The entries were barely readable.

During this research I began to suffer from an affliction I came to call "murder mind." I could work all day on my project with a certain distance, blithely looking up "bullet" or "skull" in my rhyming dictionary. But in bed at night I found a smattering of sickening images of violent acts ready and waiting for me. Reprisals of the violence done unto Jane, unto the other Michigan Murder girls, unto my loved ones, unto myself, and sometimes, most horribly, done by me. These images coursed through my mind at random intervals, but always with the slapping, prehensile force of the return of the repressed.

I persevered, mostly because I had been given an endpoint: the publication date of *Jane*, on my thirty-second birthday, in March 2005. As soon as I held the book in my hand, I would be released. I would move on to projects that had nothing to do with murder. I would never look back.

The reopening of Jane's case did away with these hopes entirely.

IN THE FALL of 2004 I moved from New York City, where I had lived for many years, to teach for a year at a college in a small town in Connecticut. The town was aptly named Middletown: in the middle of the state, in the middle of nowhere. My apartment there was beautiful—the bottom floor of a rickety 19th-century house, forty times as large as any apartment I could have afforded in New York. I set up my desk in a lovely room that my landlady introduced to me as "The Ponderosa Room"—a mahogany-paneled sunroom with three walls of windows.

In early October, about a month before Schroeder's call, I sent galleys of *Jane* to my mother for her sixtieth birthday. I was nervous; I knew the book would immerse her in the details of a story she'd been trying to put behind her for thirty-five years. More than nervous—I was terrified. As I addressed the package to her in California, it occurred to me that the book might not constitute a gift at all. If she hated it, it could be construed as a birthday-ruining disaster, a bomb, a betrayal.

I was hugely relieved when she called me after finishing the manuscript. She was in tears, saying she would be eternally grateful both to it and to me. She said it was a miracle: even though I never knew Jane, somehow I had managed to bring her back to life.

This felt like a miracle to me too. I never thought "my

Jane" might approximate the "real Jane"; I never even had designs on such a thing. But whoever "my Jane" was, she had certainly been alive with me, for me, for some time. The book's cover had been designed and pinned to my wall for months, and a defiant, androgynous, starkly lit, close-up photo of Jane's face at thirteen, taken by my grandfather, stared me down daily. The book also contained many diary entries I had culled from Jane's own writings, so copyediting the manuscript—which is what I had been doing when my mother called that November afternoon—involved paying as close attention to Jane's voice as I paid to my own.

To make sure I had her right, I had unearthed Jane's original journals, and it was not unusual that fall to find me sitting on the dark wood floor of the Ponderosa Room in a sea of pages filled with her elegant handwriting. In returning to them I was newly struck by their tormented insecurity (often manifesting itself in torrents of rhetorical, self-reprimanding questions), which contrasts starkly—sadly, even—with her obviously deep powers of articulation and feeling. This contrast runs through all her writings, from her childhood to her college years. More than runs through them—it is their very engine. It was, in fact, what made me want to write about her in the first place, as much as, or more than, the weird and awful circumstances of her death.

Never be afraid to contradict yourself. But what is there to contradict? Could I after all be very stupid—and very wrong? You're a good kid, Jane. Good for what? Who am I to judge? What was 1965? What's

been learned? What's been gained? Lost? Loved?
Hated? What do you really think? How do you explain
yourself? Why don't I ever know what I'm going to be
tomorrow? What right have we to happiness?

I recognized myself here, although I did not want to. I
would have rather chalked Jane's self-doubting agonies up
to the conundrum of growing up an effusive, probing,
ambitious girl in the sedate, patriarchal '50s—a conundrum
that several decades of feminism were supposed to have
dissolved and washed away by the time I came across her
words.

And now a detective had called to say that there had
been a DNA match in her case, and they were sure they'd
found the right guy—a retired nurse who had nothing to do
with John Norman Collins, the man who was convicted in
1970 of the final Michigan Murder, and whom most had
always assumed responsible for all. Schroeder told us that
this new suspect was now under surveillance, and would be
arrested within a few weeks. They had every reason to
believe that the case would then move swiftly toward a successful conclusion.

Leiterman was in fact taken into custody on the charge
of open murder on the day before Thanksgiving, 2004, and
then held, without bail, until his trial, which began on July
11, 2005, and ended on July 22, 2005. But over these eight
months, the dread that had accompanied my initial forays
into Jane's story did not dissipate.

It shape-shifted. It grew.

• • •

As WINTER descended in Middletown, the sunroom became the snowroom, and murder mind was back. In the morning I would pretend to know how to teach Shakespeare to fresh-faced undergraduates, then return home to talk on the phone to homicide cops and sift through the stack of books I'd checked out from the university's Science Library to try to keep up with the developments in Jane's case: *DNA for Dummies*, clinical psychology textbooks with titles like *Sexual Murder: Catathymic and Compulsive Homicides*. I flipped through the case studies in *Sexual Murder* only once but still felt as though they might have given me a fatal disease. At night I often found myself up late, unable to sleep, pacing around the Ponderosa Room in my pale blue bathrobe, a tinkling glass of whiskey and ice in my hand, watching the snow mount menacingly around the windows. I began to feel like a ghost, a stranger to myself. It wasn't quite as bad as *The Shining*, but sometimes it felt close. At least Jack Nicholson had a family to witness and rue his descent. At more jocular moments I felt like John Berryman—a throwback, a poet trapped in a gothic college town, some scraggly miscreant academic who went to dreary parties, swapped wives, and occasionally defecated, blind drunk, on a colleague's lawn. Except that in Middletown there were no such parties.

In short the ideal of catharsis that had served as a naive but real spur throughout my writing of *Jane* began to crack at the seams, and reveal itself as the ruse I had suspected it to be all along. My identification with my aunt—which had been the main thread of *Jane*, and which was arguably a result of mistaken identity on the part of my grandfather, who has called me "Jane" instead of "Maggie" for as long as I can remember—began to feel like either a hoax or a horror. I had started writing *Jane* with the presumption that my family's repression of her awful death was an example of faulty grieving, which my book could delicately expose as an unhealthy vestige of a Midwestern, Scandinavian heritage—a grim Ingmar Bergman scenario getting played out in the small, lakeside town of Muskegon, Michigan—and that I could offer a more successful model in its place.

The hubris of this idea is now abundantly clear to me. When I think now about "faulty" or "successful" grieving, I feel only bewilderment. Beyond the bewilderment, the edge of a shapeless, potent rage—a rollicking protest, some loose, hot, wild event starting to take place under my skin.

Photo #1:

A ring of male detectives standing around the shrouded lump of Jane's dead body. Taken from behind the chain-link fence, looking into Denton Cemetery. The picture cuts off around the men's waists, so all you see of them is a row of trench coat bottoms and matching black shoes. Jane's body lies at their feet, her head and upper body shrouded by her raincoat. One of her arms strays out from under it, ghostly white, flung above her head, as if she were not dead, just completely exhausted.

An Inheritance

IN ONE OF HIS last psychoanalytic papers, D. W. Winnicott wrote: *Fear of breakdown is the fear of a breakdown that has already been experienced.* This statement has always been a source of great comfort to me. For years I took it to mean that the other shoe has already dropped, that you've already been to the place you fear the most, that you've already come back from it.

It's only lately that I've realized that Winnicott is not suggesting that breakdowns do not recur. Now I see that he may be suggesting just the opposite: that a fear of breakdown in our past may be precisely what causes it to repeat in our future.

TO GET HOME to Muskegon for her spring break in late March 1969, Jane requested a ride via the campus ride board at the University of Michigan. She was going home to announce her engagement to her boyfriend, Phil, a professor of economics and fellow campus activist. Knowing her parents would not approve, she was going home alone to give them time to adjust to the news before Phil joined her a few days later. Over the telephone she arranged for a ride with a man who, unbeknownst to her, was using an alias. Phil said good-bye to her around 6:30 P.M. in her room at the Law Quad; her dead body was found about fourteen miles outside of Ann Arbor the following morning. She died from two gunshots to the head—one in her left temple, the other in her lower left skull. After she was dead, or fast approaching death, she was strangled viciously with a stocking that did not belong to her. Her body was dragged onto a stranger's grave in a small, rural cemetery called Denton Cemetery, at the end of a gravel road known locally as a "lover's lane." Her jumper was pulled up, her pantyhose pulled down, her belongings meticulously arranged between her legs and around her body, which was then covered with her raincoat and abandoned.

After Jane's murder—which was the third in a series of seven—my mother began to worry that she might be the next victim. As the case went unsolved, she kept worrying. Even visiting her sister's grave was a fraught enterprise, as the police had told the family that Jane's murderer might visit also. To mourn Jane was literally to risk encountering her killer.

Writing *Jane,* I realized this fear had trickled down to me also. An inheritance. I also knew from years of watching movies that the female detective—or, another favorite, the female professor—always has to pay for her curiosity and toughness by becoming the target of the killer himself. *One man is copying the most notorious killers in history. One at a time. Together, two women must stop him from killing again. Or they're next,* reads the tagline for the 1995 serial-killer flick *Copycat*, starring Sigourney Weaver as an alcoholic, agoraphobic professor of "serial killer studies" and Holly Hunter as her counterpart, the tough female dick.

I tried to find a sense of humor about the cinematic, self-aggrandizing images I had of discovering some crucial piece of evidence that the "professionals" had overlooked, or of someday reading from *Jane* at a bookstore with her killer clandestinely seated in the audience. I reminded myself that Jane's murderer might well have been John Collins, and told myself that even if Collins hadn't done it, her murderer might no longer be alive—or if he was, he was likely in prison for something else. Or, even if he was alive and free, the chances were close to nil that he would ever find his way to a book of poetry, even if my aunt's picture were on the cover. It was one of the few moments in my life in which poetry's obscure cultural status felt heartening.

Any two-bit shrink, or fellow writer, could have pointed out that the danger I feared from my aunt's phantom murderer—along with my closet hope that my project might somehow conjure him up—was but an extreme, ready-made metaphor for all the wild hopes and fears that can accompany the act of writing itself, especially writing about family stories that one's family would rather leave untouched, untold. Several did, in fact, point this out.

That all seemed true enough, until Schroeder called and collapsed the metaphor.

· · ·

13

WHEN *JANE* COMES out in March 2005, Schroeder will go through each poem with a highlighter. We will correspond about some details—where I got the information about the timing of a phone call Jane supposedly made on the night of her murder, if I know where he might find the guest book from Jane's funeral that I mention, and so on.

I can honestly say that it's the first book of poetry I've ever read, he will write.

I will write back, equally honestly, that it's the first I've ever written to be highlighted by a homicide detective.

IN THE WEEKS leading up to Leiterman's arrest, I couldn't stop myself from asking Schroeder if he thought Leiterman posed any danger to me or my family. It was an embarrassing question; it seemed to hoist years of pent-up irrationality into the light of day. But it was more discomfiting to think that a man who had been the object of generations of family fear was now getting up each morning, chatting with his family, and going about his daily business with no clue of his imminent arrest, or of the daily flurry of phone calls now taking place between my family and the Michigan State Police. The police had also made it clear that under no circumstances could he find out about the investigation, for fear he might flee, injure himself, or injure another.

Schroeder answered me kindly. He told me not to worry—that Leiterman was like a down-and-out Santa Claus with a bad heart and a fierce addiction to painkillers. *Let's just say he's not going to be climbing through any windows.* He added that although he, Schroeder, hadn't met me yet, he'd be willing to bet that at the very least, I would be able to outrun the guy.

IF YOU WERE to ask my mother a few years ago how Jane's murder affected the upbringing of her two daughters, she would have said that it did not. In a television interview that she and I eventually granted to a show from CBS, *48 Hours Mystery*, during Leiterman's trial, my mother told the attractive, busty interviewer that she thought she had always been too "in control" to allow her sister's death to affect her behavior in any substantive way. The realization that she may not have been as "in control" as she imagined—a realization delivered, in part, by reading *Jane*, which chronicles the many years she spent barricading doors, etc.—startled her.

My mother remains equally startled by the fact that her body gets hungry, has to go to the bathroom, or reacts to environmental factors such as altitude or temperature. She dreams of an impermeable, self-sufficient body, one not subject to uncontrollable needs or desires, be they its own or those of others. She dreams of a body that cannot be injured, violated, or sickened unless it chooses to be.

Recently my mother tripped while speaking to my sister Emily on the phone. She fell to the ground in her kitchen, and her tooth smashed up against her upper lip. Her lip was swollen beyond recognition for weeks, and the tooth died; eventually she had to have a root canal. On the phone, my sister had no idea that she had fallen, because our mother talked right through it. When Emily and I bug her about this cover-up after the fact, she protests, *What purpose could it possibly have served to tell Emily that I'd had an accident? She couldn't have helped me, and it only would have made her worry.*

She says the fall was too embarrassing to mention. I say that it might have been worth mentioning simply because it happened. We may as well be talking to each other from opposite ends of a cardboard tube.

By the time my mother and I find ourselves at the *48 Hours* interview, seated side by side in a wainscoted room at the U of M Law School that CBS has taken over for the shoot and lined with fruit, coffee, and cookies, it is the last day of Lieterman's trial, and we will have spent weeks looking at autopsy photos of Jane projected on a big screen in the courtroom. I will have started to understand where my mother's fantasy of a sovereign, impermeable self might have come from.

A medical examiner had described each of these photos out loud at the January hearing. There was no jury then, and thus no need for projected pictures. As the examiner spoke, tears streamed involuntarily from my eyes, from my sister's eyes. But my mother did not cry. Her body simply collapsed in on itself. Her shoulders rounded over, her chest hollowed out, her whole body becoming more and more of a husk. Her knees shaking in spasms. I wanted to touch her but I didn't know what kind of touch would help. First I tried pressing my hands down lightly on the top of her shaking thighs, then I put a hand to her back. She did not respond to either. It was clear that she had entered a world beyond touch, a world beyond comfort.

My sister and I escaped to the bathroom at a break, and there Emily told me that she could barely look at our mother. She simply could not bear to see her in so much pain. I agreed, but did not confess to the less-admirable emotion. I also felt angry. I wanted our mother to meet these details with squared shoulders. I couldn't bear the way this man's words were shriveling her body into that of a little girl. I didn't want her to turn away; I didn't want her to shake. As I watched my beautiful sister wash and dry her hands and apply lipstick I tried to imagine how I'd feel if I were looking at autopsy photos of her on a big screen instead of Jane; the thought brought a quick flash of guilt and paralysis, followed by a wave of nausea. This was my mother's sister. What was I expecting?

You never saw such a wild thing as my mother, her hat seized by the winds and blown out to sea so that her hair was her white mane, her black lisle legs exposed to the thigh, her skirts tucked round her waist, one hand on the reins of the rearing horse while the other clasped my father's service revolver and, behind her, the breakers of the savage, indifferent sea, like the witnesses of a furious justice, writes Angela Carter in her retelling of the Bluebeard myth.

In Carter's version of the story, Bluebeard does not murder his young bride. Instead her mother arrives in the nick of time and puts "a single, irreproachable bullet" through Bluebeard's head.

Is this what I was hoping for?

The Face of Evil

He has come to gas the house and I am chained into a large birdcage that clangs against everything when I walk around. I'm trying to get up the stairs in the cage but it's hard. He acted very affectionate and kind when he came to gas the house and yet I knew he was going to kill me. Clearly he is deranged. I clang my way out of the house, noticing that he has duct-taped all the vents, etc. I burst out onto a lawn which slopes down into mud, toward a river. The mud feels amazingly green and wet and good, very real. I know instantly that the mud is the savior, the mud is the antidote to the poison gas. Later when he comes back he tries to act unsurprised that I am still alive, but he is obviously quite surprised. I hog-tie him and put him in a black garbage bag and go to burn him alive. I am thinking, I know this is only a dream, but am I really going to let myself do all these aggressive and violent things? I muse for a moment on how heavy the bag will probably be because he is such a big guy, but being a dream it doesn't give me any problem. Once he is tied up and in the bag he doesn't make any noise anymore, it's like he's ceased to exist.

AND SO I HAVE dreamt for years of confronting some sinister, composite epitome of male violence and power, the murderer I always presumed to be Jane's. Sometimes he is a faceless shadow; other times he has the face of someone I know. Sometimes my mother and sister are there, and we help each other. Other times we are all there but we don't help each other, either because we can't or we won't. Most often I am alone.

My only other image of Jane's potential murderer was that of John Collins, who, at the time of his arrest, was a young, handsome white boy, and apparently quite the charmer. *Lucky with the ladies,* as they say.

HOLDING HANDS, sitting side by side on our bench at the January hearing, my mother, Emily, and I now watch an overweight, bespectacled, sixty-two-year-old man in a forest-green prison jumpsuit shuffle into the courtroom. He is mostly bald, with white, craggy hair in a crescent shape, and a face full of whiskers, which he runs his hands over frequently. He has a large, bulbous nose that occasionally flushes dark red, and small, stunned eyes. Under the defense table, his feet lie flat against the floor, shackled at the ankles, in black socks and plastic brown prison sandals. Periodically he takes off his glasses and cleans them with the edge of his green prison shirt, then squints back out at the courtroom. The few times he turns around to scan the entire room he looks completely disoriented, as if he has no idea where he is.

I feel disoriented too. Where I imagined I might find the "face of evil," I am finding the face of Elmer Fudd.

On this day Leiterman spends a lot of time watching his hands, which for the most part stay in a steepled position in front of his face or against his swollen belly. I am reminded of his nursing career by the way he shoots into action when anyone in the courtroom needs to put on latex gloves to handle evidence. Otherwise fairly motionless, he quickly picks up the box of powdered gloves and shakes it out to witnesses or lawyers whenever they need them, often a moment before the need arises, with a nurse's instinct for protection. In the late afternoon a deep shaft of sunlight moves over the courtroom, and eventually lands on the defense table. Everyone else shifts positions or moves seats to get out of it, but Leiterman cannot move, he has to abide it. I watch the sun saturate his face and body, watch him shield his face with his hands in vain. Just as he instinctively offers up the gloves, I feel the urge to shield him, to block the sun with my body, or at least pull down a shade.

We stay planted in our positions; I watch the light move over him.

I watch the light and I watch his hands and I try to imagine them around the trigger of a gun, I try to imagine them strangling someone. Strangling Jane. I know this kind of imagining is useless and awful. I wonder how I'd feel if I imagined it over and over again and later found out that he didn't do it. I stare at him all day as if a sign were about to come down from the heavens to indicate his guilt or innocence. It doesn't come.

The purpose of the January hearing is to lay out the bare bones of the case before a judge: to prove that a homicide was committed, to confirm that the victim was Jane, to offer enough probable cause to warrant a full trial, to determine whether Leiterman should remain in custody until that trial, and if so, to post or deny bail, and so on. On this day my grandfather is the first witness called to the stand. Everyone in the courtroom worries a bit as he totters in and out of the witness box; it seems an especially cruel moment to bust a hip.

Once on the stand he looks ancient. He is wearing a favorite royal purple blazer and a bright red cashmere sweater that my mother gave him for Christmas a few weeks earlier. The state's attorney, Steven Hiller, asks him to please tell the court what he saw at the morgue on the afternoon of March 21, 1969. My grandfather leans forward and says clearly: *It was my second-born daughter.* He still looks amazed.

At the end of this day my grandfather announces that he has a "gut feeling" about Leiterman. He announces this at dinner at the Olive Garden in the strip mall across the freeway from the motel where the state has put us all up for the night. He mentions this "gut feeling" several times, but never says exactly what it is.

All I'm saying is that he looks like a tortured man, he says.

I don't expect you to have empathy for the guy, Schroeder had told me the day after Leiterman's arrest. *I mean, he's a sorry sack of shit. But he's in hideous health, and, in my opinion, his body is completely eaten up by the things he's done.*

Sitting at the Olive Garden, I wonder, does looking like a tortured man or having an eaten-up body mean that you premeditated and carried out the brutal, sexualized murder of a complete stranger three decades ago? I am also now remembering that when I tentatively, covertly interviewed my grandfather for *Jane* a few years back, he said that he had a "gut feeling" about John Collins.

Although in his nineties, my grandfather shows few to no signs of fatigue, either with daily life or with the nine decades of it prior. He drinks about three pots of coffee a day, and takes hot baths and does crossword puzzles throughout the night. The prosecution team calls him "Dr. Dan," which suits him well; he was a practicing dentist for more than sixty years. He wants to be sharp as a tack and he is. And yet I know he gets tired, because in court he falls asleep a multitude of times, his head slumping onto the shoulder of whichever family member happens to be sitting beside him. Each time he wakes up he appears alarmed, and immediately reassures the dead courtroom air, *I'm all right, I'm all right.*

In the months leading up to the July trial, he will become increasingly concerned that the police are going to suggest exhuming Jane's body from her grave in search of more evidence. He starts calling my mother late at night to say he won't allow it, he simply won't allow it.

My mother tells him not to be paranoid. *We'll cross that bridge when we come to it,* she says. So far we have not come to it.

A Live Stream

O<small>N THAT JANUARY</small> day Hiller warned us that the medical examiner's testimony was but a warm-up for the graphic nature of the trial to come. Before he began his opening arguments on July 12, 2005, he warned us again. He took the members of Jane's family who were present that day—me, my mother, my grandfather, Jane's younger brother and his wife—aside in the courtroom hallway to tell us that he would be projecting several photos from Jane's autopsy for the jury, photos that we might not want to see.

My uncle heeds the warning, says he can't think of one good reason to have those images in his mind, and heads straight down to the courthouse coffee shop.

My mother feels differently. *We're tough,* she tells Hiller. *We can take it.* I'm not sure for whom she's speaking.

My grandfather seems distraught, stranded between the polar stances of his two surviving children. He turns to me and asks, *What do you think I should do, kiddo?*

I think you should do exactly what you need to do, I say inanely, knowing full well that he has no idea what he needs to do, and that he's not going to be able to figure it out in the two minutes he has to decide before the courtroom fills up.

He shuffles in, and the slide show begins.

Photo #2:

Jane, on a metal gurney. A profile shot, from the sternum upwards. She is naked, except for a baby-blue headband, which is thin, just a little more than a ribbon. Her hair is auburn and shiny with blood. And then, tied around her neck, almost like another fashion accessory, like some perverse ascot, is the stocking that was used to strangle her, its knot and two ends streaming toward the camera. The stocking looks reddish, probably from the age of the photo. As far as I know it was just a plain brown stocking. Not hers. "An import into the scene," as they say. Embedded so deeply and wrongly into her skin that it appears here as a cartoon. Her face and shoulder and armpit are luminous, light sources unto themselves. Her armpit looks especially white and tender, like the armpit of a little girl. An armpit that's never seen the sun.

After the first few photos, Hiller comes over to our bench. He whispers to us that the next is particularly gruesome, that we might not want to see it.

It shows Jane's neck after the stocking was removed, he whispers. *The furrow is quite deep.*

My mother repeats this information to my grandfather, who is sitting to her right and whose hearing isn't good enough to make out the low decibel of Hiller's whisper.

He says we might not want to see this one, my mother says into his ear. *The furrow is quite deep.*

Huh? my grandfather asks, *what's that?*

YOU MIGHT NOT WANT TO LOOK AT THIS ONE, she repeats in a stage whisper as she lowers her head toward her knees.

On her way down she whispers to me, *Tell me if I should look.*

With my mother bent over I feel suddenly exposed on the bench, the sole bird left on a wire. I just sit there dumbly staring at the screen, waiting for the next image to come up, feeling about as able to control what I allow in as an antenna.

I am developing little methods, however. Each time an image appears I look at it quickly, opening and closing my eyes like a shutter. Then I look a little longer, in increments, until my eyes can stay open. I know the image will stay on the screen for some time, until the attorneys and their witnesses have said everything about it that needs to be said. So there's no rush. You can acclimate to it slowly. And the thing is, you do acclimate.

Well? my mother whispers from her bent-over pose.

It's not so bad, I whisper back, *but you might as well not look.*

AS WE FILE out of court at the end of this day, my grandfather slaps my mother's and my backs and says confidently, *Well,* that *didn't hurt us.*

I have no idea what he's talking about.

Speak for yourself, I want to say.

27

Or, *That's what you think now—but just you wait.*

Or, *What do you mean by "hurt"? What does "hurt" mean to you?*

I hold him up on one side as we descend the stairs, and he holds on to the railing on the other. At the bottom he hugs me closer and says, *You know you'll always be my Janie.*

Jesus, Grandpa, I want to say. *Did you see how your Janie looked in there? She didn't look so good.*

But I just nod, as the automatic doors of the courthouse swing open, and deliver us back out into the oppressive summer heat.

COURT TV later reported:

> As the washed-out pictures were flashed onto a large projection screen, jurors appeared solemn. A few women on the panel looked toward the victim's relatives, seated in the front row of the courtroom. On three separate occasions, Hiller approached the family to warn them that he was about to show disturbing pictures, but each time, Dan Mixer, the victim's ninety-year-old father, replied, "I'll stay."

THE PERSON WHO first discovered Jane's body on the morning of March 21, 1969, was a young housewife named Nancy Grow. I had read about this woman and her discovery in many different places over the years—in *The Michi-*

gan Murders, for example, she makes a cameo appearance as "Penny Stowe." I had also written a poem about her in *Jane.* I never dreamed of seeing her in the flesh.

Now in her sixties—birdlike, restrained, her nerves taut under her skin—Grow resurfaces at the January hearing to describe her encounter with Jane's body over three decades ago. She does not seem happy to do so. Nonetheless, she politely explains how her son brought her a bloodstained bag he'd found on his way to the school bus, how she shooed him off, then took a look around her street. She walked over to Denton Cemetery, stopped outside its chain-link fence, and stood there at Jane's feet, paralyzed with horror. She can't recall how long she stood there, staring. She kept thinking, *Maybe it's a dummy, maybe it's a dummy.* At some point she walked a few feet into the cemetery, past the fence, to get a better view. Then, wearing just her nightgown and loafers, she ran to her car and drove to her sister's house a few blocks away. She began screaming uncontrollably as soon as she got there.

Grow didn't think she absorbed anything at all about Jane's specific features at the time, but surprised herself later by being able to pick Jane's face out of a yearbook. *Her face stayed with me,* she says.

Grow admits that she never told the police that she crossed the fence and went into the cemetery. When an attorney asks her why, she says she felt too ashamed. She can't say why, but she felt ashamed.

Watching this soft-spoken, traumatized woman on the stand, who steadfastly avoids looking at my family and instead stares down at her hands for the majority of her testimony, I begin to feel ashamed, too.

Grow felt ashamed then for stepping in to take a closer look. Perhaps she feels ashamed now because it can feel hard and wrong to talk about the suffering of a stranger in the presence of those who knew and loved her.

I know both of these feelings well. I have been taking a closer look for some time. And although Jane and I are connected by blood, she remains as much of a stranger to me as she was to Grow. The story of her death may have affected both of our lives and brought us into the same room, but that doesn't mean that either of us feels that it's ours to tell.

Grow's shame at the January hearing will set her apart from almost everyone else at the July trial. No one else will seem to have any—not the medical examiner who compares the body temperature taken in Jane's rectum at the crime scene against that taken from the center of her liver during her autopsy; not the middle-aged true-crime writer from Australia who sits on the bench in front of ours every day, taking notes for a book; not the dowdy journalist from the local paper who lurks in a bathroom stall in the ladies' room to eavesdrop on my mother's and my conversations; none of the cameramen who film us walking in and out of the courthouse day after day, our faces wrinkled with sleep in the morning, then tear-stained and haggard by evening; none of the producers from *48 Hours*, who will make heavy use of the crime scene photos in their show, and who had planned to use the autopsy photos as well until Hiller stepped in to say absolutely not; none of the Court TV correspondents, who will stream the autopsy photos live on the Web, then keep them available to the public in an online archive.

Perhaps the shame I feel is a stand-in for the shame I think someone ought to feel.

Or perhaps it's due to the fact that during Leiterman's trial, I sat in the courtroom every day with a legal pad and pen, jotting down all the gory details, no different or better than anyone else. Details which I'm reassembling here— a live stream—for reasons that are not yet clear or justifiable to me, and may never be.

But as I told my mother after her tumble in the kitchen, some things might be worth telling simply because they happened.

The Red Parts

IN THE YEARS after my father died, I often found myself alone, or alone with my mother. *Just us chickens,* she'd say. Emily left for boarding school when she was thirteen and I was eleven, a departure that marked the start of a series of adventures and incarcerations from which she would never return home. My mother had a new husband, but his presence felt alien, intermittent. He appeared sporadically at the dinner table with hands darkened by paint and oil. He was a housepainter and carpenter several years her junior whom she and my father had hired years ago to paint our family home in San Rafael, the only house I remember living in with both my parents. My father was a lawyer who was out of town a lot in those days; my mother was a frustrated housewife at home with two small children. She fell in love with the housepainter when I was seven, divorced my father when I was eight, and married the housepainter when I was nine.

For about a year and a half after the divorce Emily and I cavorted between our parents' various apartments and homes under the rubric of "joint custody." But a phone call in the early evening on January 28, 1984, altered this structure. My father was supposed to meet a friend that afternoon, but he never showed up. The friend called my mother, said she was worried, that it was unlike him, that something about it didn't feel right. At this point my mother and father were living but a few miles away from each other in a town called Mill Valley. They were still close—in fact, my father often acted as if one day the cloud of madness would simply pass and they would get back together as if nothing had ever happened. My mother told his friend she would stop over at his house and make sure everything was OK. Emily and I went along.

Although we had no reason to suspect anything was seriously amiss, the short car ride over to his house felt ominous. Emily or I—I can't remember who—asked my mother to shut off the radio, as its manic chirping sounded all wrong. Pulling up to his house, my mother noticed that there were several newspapers in the driveway, and that the mail hadn't been taken in.

We all went inside together, but my mother went downstairs to his bedroom alone. A minute later, she was back upstairs, yelling at us to leave the house, immediately.

Emily and I sat for some time outside on the curb, watching our mother through the windows as she moved hysterically from room to room, screaming, *You can't come in until I make sure there are no signs of foul play. I need to make sure there are no signs of foul play.*

I was ten, and did not know what *foul play* meant. I knew it was the title of a Goldie Hawn/Chevy Chase movie I'd recently watched with my father on Showtime, but that movie had been a comedy.

Where does your father keep the goddamn phone book, she yelled, frantically throwing open cabinets, forgetting, in her shock, that all she had to do was dial 911.

For about a half hour Emily and I shared the darkening street with a teenage boy who skateboarded up and down the block, quizzically watching the scene unfold as dusk gave way to night. When the police and ambulance finally arrived, he clattered away.

Emily and I followed the paramedics into the house, where I took up residence in a crevice between a wine rack and couch in my father's living room. I don't know where Emily went. From my crevice I could stay out of the way but still see what was happening. First I watched the paramedics rush down the stairs to his bedroom with a stretcher. Then I watched the staircase. After what felt like a long time, I watched them come back up the staircase. They were moving much more slowly now, and carrying a stretcher as flat and empty and white as it had been on its way down.

That's when I knew he was dead, although I didn't know how or why, and I wouldn't really believe it for some time.

My mother told us later that she had found him lying perpendicular on his bed, as if he'd sat up, planted his feet on the ground, then fallen backwards. He was already cold.

I don't know how long we stayed at his house, but eventually we drove back to my mother's and stepfather's. Once there my mother fumbled around in a storage closet looking for a board game for us to play. She said that she and her family had played a board game the night after Jane was killed, and that it had helped.

I don't remember playing the game, nor do I remember it helping.

I do remember Emily swearing to me before going to sleep that night that she would never shed a single tear for our father, whom she had absolutely adored. So had I. I remember thinking at the time that her idea did not sound like a good one.

AFTER THIS night Emily and I moved in with my mother and her new husband "full time." The house they had recently purchased was perched so high up on a hill and so deep into the redwoods that in my dreams now it always appears as a fortress comprised solely of shadows and vines. It was perpetually damp and moldy, perpetually shrouded in fog. It was not unusual for my mother and I to spend an entire day chasing a single sunbeam throughout the house to sit in, then an entire evening hovering over the single heater, reading our books side by side, our clothes tented by hot air.

Emily and I shared the basement of this house for about a year, although we each had our separate rooms. Until our stepfather remodeled it the basement retained the hippie remnants of the Doobie Brothers and Santana, both of whom had allegedly passed through the house before we got there: wooden-beaded doorways, floor-to-ceiling acoustic tiling. I fought to keep one of their left-over waterbeds, a goofy, jiggly thing I slept on until I left home.

Not long after we moved in "full time," the house was burglarized, which gave it an aura of imminent danger that never diminished. The burglars came in the late afternoon, a time of day when Emily and I were usually at home alone but on this day happened to stay late at school. Conversely our stepfather had happened to come home early, and he got a good look at the guy waiting in the getaway car at the bottom of our impossibly steep and long driveway. He never saw the face of the man inside, the one who yelled from upstairs, *I have a gun, get out now.* My stepfather ended up testifying against the getaway driver in court, and was enraged when, a few months down the line, we found ourselves seated at a booth next to him at an Italian restaurant down the street.

After that, whenever I came home alone to the empty house I walked up its driveway in a slow zigzag with a deepening sense of dread. Once at the top I would let myself in with the spare key that hung on a nail on the back of a redwood post, then undertake a brief but thorough search of the house to make sure there were no intruders or dead bodies in it. This ritual involved arming myself with a butcher knife and checking the closets, beds, and bathtubs for bodies before settling in and starting my homework. Often I talked aloud during the search, telling the invisible intruder that I was onto him, that I knew he was there, that I wasn't afraid of him, not one bit.

One night out at dinner during Leiterman's trial, my

mother tells me offhandedly that she has never liked hiking because she has always been afraid that she'll come across a dead body along the trail. At first I think she's completely bonkers. Then I remember this butcher-knife ritual. Then I fast-forward to my years working at a bar off the Bowery in New York's East Village, and remember how undone I felt whenever the bathroom door was locked for a significant period of time, and an annoyed customer needing to pee would ask me to deal with it. After the obligatory loud knocking and shouts of *Hello, anybody in there,* I would unlock the door and swing it open quickly, fully expecting to find a dead body slumped over the toilet.

Ninety-five percent of the time, the door had jammed from the inside, and the bathroom would be empty, just a tiny cubicle lit by a bulb wrapped in lavender cellophane, the kind of light that makes the space look hip and also too dark to find a vein. But the other 5 percent there would be a body, of someone who had OD'd or passed out. I knew that at least one person had died of a heroin overdose in there, and while I hadn't been working that night it was enough to make the whole thing feel like Russian roulette. I dreaded breaking into the bathroom each night of the five years I worked there.

I still dream about this dim lavender bathroom. Just the other night a woman slit her wrists in there—a woman we, as bar employees, were somehow supposed to be taking care of, making sure she didn't pass out, shoot up, or hurt herself. But we fucked up, we let her get hold of a razor blade, and she locked herself in the little bathroom to die. The bathroom floor was made of metal grates; below the grates lay the molten center of the universe. She stretched out against the metal and let her blood spill down to the earth's core, spraying the churning underworld with her fluids. As a courtesy she had wadded cotton into the porous parts of the brick walls beforehand. When we pulled the cotton out, torrents of her blood flooded the bar.

The irony of this fear was that my apartment on the Lower East Side was itself a dope pit. When I got home from work late at night I had to check my roommate's room for nodded-out, dopesick girls whose cigarettes might be burning holes in his furniture before I could go to sleep. More than once I'd wiped up weird white crud foaming out of his insensate mouth. Since I didn't use, I never really knew what to do—I just wiped up the crud, made sure all the cigarettes were out, checked that everyone was breathing, and went to sleep.

The truth was that my bed was a dope pit as well. In it I had come across the overdosed body of my junkie boyfriend on more than one occasion. The last of these times, after I had called 911 and hauled him to St. Vincent's, I realized—at long last—that I might be in over my head. After getting him admitted I went outside in the pouring rain and called my mother from a pay phone. I was mortified but didn't know what else to do. I hadn't told her anything about the situation, hadn't told her about finding his blue-gray body over and over again like so much dead meat in my bed, hadn't told her about the nights of getting alcoholic hives and hyperventilating in the bathroom while he packed powder against the fingernail of his pinky, saying *This is the perfect amount for you, for small you.*

In the ambulance, when he came to, he said, *I think I've killed my tongue,* as if speaking through a cord of foam.

I'm outside a hospital, I told her. *It's pouring. I think I have to get out of here.*

She listened for a while, then said, *Well, what would Jesus do?*

She wasn't kidding. She's not even religious. She was probably just influenced by something she was reading.

Jesus wouldn't walk away, she said. *Try to see the evening through.*

He's going to die this time, I said.

All the more reason.

I was a complete fool then, but not so complete of a fool that I didn't know, on some level, what I was doing. As the doctor attached electrodes to his chest, got his heartbeat to stabilize, and pronounced, *He's going to be fine,* I felt an outsized relief flood through my body, along with a swell of pride. Ten years meant nothing. It was the night of my father's death, but this time I'd arrived at his house in time, this time I was an adult and had all the skills to make it right.

But "making it right" did not bring my father back. It just had me signing hospital release papers for a terrible junkie, who staggered home with me like a brain-dead puppy, confessed an affair with some dumb fellow junkie in the middle of the night, then went out to score at a gas station on Houston and Avenue C.

The morning after this night I stayed in bed all day. I pretended I was one of those children with that disease where their bones shatter into a million pieces if they move too quickly or come into contact with anyone. I was sick, like the-boy-in-the-bubble. I took a medium-sized bottle of Jim Beam and drank from it under the covers while reading *No Man Is an Island* by Thomas Merton.

> Without God, we are no longer persons. We become dumb animals under pain, happy if we can behave at least like quiet animals and die without too much confusion.

For the first time in my life I felt paralyzed thinking about Christ. I dragged the phone into the nest of my bed and called an old writing teacher who was famous for being a religious zealot. *A Christian intellectual,* she said. I told her I had seen an article she had recently published about Luke, I couldn't remember where, could she send it to me, could she at least tell me what it had said?

Why not just read the red parts on your own? she said.

OK, I told her, hanging up. *I'll do that.*

I had no idea what she meant. I felt stupid then, but nearly everyone I've asked since hasn't known either. In graduate school years later I even asked a professor of "textual scholarship" at a lecture and he just shrugged. At the time I imagined slitting a body from chin to genitals, spreading apart its internal organs and trying to read them like tea leaves.

Just a few days later I witnessed from the window of this apartment the only murder I've yet to see. I woke up at 5 A.M. to the sound of a man running and a car screeching and looked out just in time to see three Chinese gang members whack the running man in the head with a baseball bat, then jump in their car and drive away. They had whacked him hard. A minute later an old Chinese woman in her nightgown ran down the block screaming, the thin plastic soles of her shoes flapping against the cobblestones, echoing. All of this happened in purplish morning light, the light that grows before dawn between the blackened tenements and the East River. The woman knelt down by his body, which was lying at a strange angle in the gutter, and cradled him. The amount of blood leaving his head was tremendous. I called 911 and they said, *Were the assailants black or Hispanic. Neither,* I said, and didn't give my name. By 8 A.M. people were opening up their stores along Orchard Street, walking over the rust-colored stain on the sidewalk without seeing it, without knowing anything had ever happened there. By midafternoon the stain was gone.

Write the things which thou hast seen, and the things which are, and the things which shall be, hereafter. A red part.

Addendum

As *JANE* WAS going to print in the winter of 2004, I pondered writing an addendum that would announce the developments in her case. Schroeder had suggested it jokingly when we first spoke on the phone. My mother had told him about my forthcoming book, and, while he was intrigued by it, he wanted to make sure that I didn't say anything in public about it before Leiterman had been arrested. I assured him that the book wouldn't be out for months, and that poetry wasn't a mass-market kind of a thing.

Even so, he said, *you'd better get ready to write an addendum. An addendum that explains everything.*

On November 12, 2004, I sat down at my desk in the Ponderosa Room, took out a piece of paper, and wrote at the top of the page:

FIRST ATTEMPT AT AN ADDENDUM
THAT EXPLAINS EVERYTHING

The addendum took the form of a list:

1. In 2001, around the time I started writing this book, unbeknownst to me, the box of evidence

pertaining to Jane's murder was removed from its storage locker and sent to the state crime lab in Lansing, Michigan, for genetic testing.

2. Much of the genetic material found on the objects in the box—such as a large bloodstain on a yellow-and-white striped towel left at the crime scene, for example—presumably came from Jane herself. But certain pieces of evidence yielded foreign DNA, primarily in the form of cellular deposits found on several sites on Jane's pantyhose.

3. These cellular deposits were not from blood, semen, urine, or feces. They came from an unidentifiable source—the lab analyst is currently guessing it's sweat. Wherever they came from, the analyst says there are copious amounts of them. "A mother lode."

4. On July 7, 2004, CODIS—the Combined DNA Index System, a computer database overseen by the FBI which compares DNA samples from convicted felons against evidentiary samples submitted by labs around the country—notified Lansing that foreign DNA cells from sampled sites #1–3 on Jane's pantyhose had returned a cold hit, to a man by the name of Gary Earl Leiterman.

5. Gary Earl Leiterman is a retired nurse who lives with his wife of many years, Solly, in a lakeside home in Pine Grove Township near Gobles, Michigan. He and Solly have two grown, adopted

children, who are his wife's sister's children, both
from the Philippines.

6. Leiterman's DNA entered CODIS due to a 2001
   felony charge for forging narcotics prescriptions.
   He was arrested for using blank prescription forms
   from Borgess Medical Center, the hospital where
   he worked for many years, to obtain the painkiller
   Vicodin from a local Meijer's. He was sentenced to
   drug rehab. Beyond this, he has no criminal record.

7. Putting aside, for the moment, the many factors
   that can complicate statistical inferences, the odds
   that the "mother lode" of cellular material on Jane's
   pantyhose could have come from someone other
   than Leiterman are roughly 171.7 trillion to one.

The list could have ended there, and perhaps explained
something. But it went on:

8. On December 9, 2003, about eight months before
   the hit to Leiterman came in, CODIS returned a
   different hit in Jane's case—this one to a man by
   the name of John David Ruelas.

9. The Ruelas match came not from Jane's pantyhose,
   but from a perfectly formed droplet of blood that
   was found on the back of the left hand of Jane's
   dead body back in 1969. This droplet stood out to
   a cop at the time because it was not smeared, as was
   all other blood found on her. At her autopsy an

examiner scraped this droplet into a miniature manila envelope, where it sat for the next thirty-odd years.

10. After the CODIS match to Ruelas came in, the police immediately set out to find him. They found a thirty-seven-year-old man in prison, serving out a twenty- to forty-year sentence for beating his mother, Margaret Ruelas, to death on January 25, 2002.

11. Ruelas had apparently beaten his mother for many years; his final assault left her with eleven broken ribs and her face "pounded purple."

12. On March 20, 1969, the night of Jane's murder, John David Ruelas would have been four years old.

13. From prison, Ruelas tells the police that he knows things about Jane's murder—things he will share with them if they will bargain over his sentence. But since Ruelas was only four at the time and is now desperate to plea-bargain, no one trusts a word he says. As far as getting information from his caretakers in 1969 goes, his mother is (obviously) dead; it turns out that his father, David Ruelas, was also murdered, in a separate incident, back in the '70s. His father was killed with a hammer, rolled up in a carpet doused with gasoline, set on fire, and tossed into a dumpster. That case also remains unsolved.

14. In a conference call with my family, the detectives admit that the match to John Ruelas is bizarre and disturbing. But, given the science, they say they

have no choice but to believe that the little boy somehow "came into contact" with Jane's body on the night of her murder. In 1969 the Ruelas family was living in downtown Detroit—about thirty-five miles from Denton Cemetery, i.e., not exactly around the corner. (Leiterman, on the other hand, was living nearby.) But the detectives say that the idea that "little Johnny" might have been involved in Jane's murder in some way isn't as far-fetched as it might initially sound, given the "circumstances of his home life." They do not elaborate, except to say that they know that Johnny was a childhood nosebleeder.

Looking over this list, I realize I cannot include it in *Jane.* In fact, I can barely share it with my friends, much less with strangers. I learn quickly that it does not make good cocktail conversation. Not only that, but it explains virtually nothing.

In all the permutations of murder mind that I had experienced, I had never imagined a scenario involving a child. Now I found myself pacing the Ponderosa Room in my bathrobe late at night with my thoughts swirling strangely and dreadfully around the question of how a four-year-old boy might have "come into contact" with Jane's body. Or more specifically, how a drop of his blood could have ended up on the back of her hand.

I read this story yesterday and I'm still banging my head against the wall, writes a blogger on a criminal law Web site, responding to an article announcing the double DNA match in Jane's case.

At a hearing in May 2005, a judge will ask Hiller how the state plans on explaining the presence of Ruelas's blood in trial.

There's a world of possibilities, Hiller will say.

Name one, the judge will snap back.

THE BIG MOVIE playing all season at the theater in downtown Middletown is *Seed of Chucky,* the fifth install-ment of a string of slasher comedies about a killer doll. Daily I pass by its poster, which features a bloodstained toddler in a striped shirt and white overalls, his demented face held together by stitches. I almost want to go see it.

EVENTUALLY other bloggers, some as far away as Aus-tralia or the U.K., start to weigh in:

Perhaps the 4 year old was indeed at the crime scene somehow. Or, perhaps the profile identification is a false hit. In the former case, it is spooky and tragic; in the latter it is, perhaps, a crack in the idea that DNA (done right) is infallible.

Interesting, and ultimately depressing, story . . . As for what could be an apparent 4 year old co-murderer, that might almost make an interesting anthology. Here's

the scenario, what is each writer's solution? The fact
that it's twisted enough for me to even have that
thought depresses me even more.

Something does not seem right in this reopening of
her murder.

The defense agrees. It will argue that the reason why
there is no discernible link between Leiterman, Ruelas, and
Jane is that there is none—save the fact that genetic samples from all three people were being processed in the
same DNA laboratory over the same period of time in
early 2002. It's true: bloody clothing from Ruelas's 2002
murder of his mother was being tested in the Lansing lab
on at least one of the same days that an analyst was working on the blood droplet scraped off Jane's hand in 1969.
And individual samples from Leiterman and Ruelas were
both brought into the lab in early 2002 under a new Michigan law that went into effect on January 1, 2002, which
required all convicted felons—violent and nonviolent
alike—to provide DNA samples to CODIS.

One too many coincidences, Leiterman's lawyer will say.

All spring I meticulously cut out articles from the *New
York Times* about DNA lab scandals in Houston, in Mary-
land. In the Houston lab some evidence was stored so
poorly that one observer saw blood leaking out of a cardboard evidence box after a heavy rain. Laboratory contamination seems a more likely—not to mention a more
wholesome—scenario than any of the others I can imagine.

The boy was forced to watch. The boy witnessed it, inadvertently. Somehow the boy was forced to take part in it. He was forced to cause harm. The boy shed blood; maybe there was a fight. Maybe the boy was hurt and bleeding before he arrived at the scene. Leiterman knew his family, and he killed her at their house. For some reason the boy was in his car. The boy was wandering, on his own, and came across Jane's body in the cemetery. The boy stood above her dead or dying body, horrified, confused, uncomprehending, as a single drop of blood dripped from his nose onto her hand.

Eventually I make a rule that I can only think about "the Ruelas question"—sometimes referred to as the "lost boy theory"—while swimming laps in the university pool. It seems right to think about it underwater.

Here's the scenario, what is each writer's solution?

Something does not seem right in this reopening of her murder.

Red House

At my mother's and stepfather's, up the dark hill. Emily and her much-older boyfriend are making out in the basement. He yells upstairs to my mother, "I'm finger-fucking your daughter"—my mother doesn't make him leave. I yell something about there being more discipline in the home. But I yell too loudly, and Mom is frail—she has a heart attack in Emily's room. I yell to Emily, "Call 911." Mom's on the floor now, I'm cradling her. Instead of calling 911, Emily asks her, "Do you want to go out to a club?" She thinks this is hilarious; I'm furious that she isn't helping. I know her boyfriend is violent, I know he's hit my sister, so I let him punch me in the face, just to prove I'm not afraid. "You don't scare me," I say, then do some aikido on him, which shrinks him into a little boy.

E MILY LEFT FOR her freshman year of boarding school pregnant. Our mother did not know this, nor did Emily herself, until she was throwing up with regularity in her morning chemistry class. We discussed the situation on the phone—she from the pay phone in her new dorm, me still in the basement.

Imagine how surprised Mom would be if the baby came out white instead of black, she laughed roughly. Her nineteen-year-old boyfriend was black, but she figured that the responsible party was more likely the oldest son of a (white) friend of our mother's—a good-looking, skinny kid who had purportedly punched his equally skinny, glassine mother in the stomach on more than one occasion. One night over at their house for dinner, while my mother and her friend exchanged confidences over wine upstairs, Emily had sex with the boy on the lower bunk bed in his bedroom while, in the adjacent room, his younger, much less good-looking brother threw frogs from his frog collection at my legs in an attempt to stun them.

That means he likes you, their mother winked at me when the four of us finally surfaced for dinner, Emily rumpled, me with mud-spattered calves.

I found the secret of Emily's pregnancy hard to keep. She seemed to be hoping that within time the problem would just go away. She was also dropping a lot of acid, and I worried that the fetus was becoming a kind of spangled, brain-damaged alien.

Eventually she told our mother; eventually there was an abortion. I don't remember anything about that weekend except that when they got home from the doctor Emily bolted out of the car holding her stomach, ran into the house and straight to her bedroom, her face red and bloated from tears.

By the spring she had been expelled, having racked up three "major incidents" at a school with a three-strikes-and-you're-out policy.

It turned out that my mother and her husband could also keep a secret, for just a few months later, they ambushed Emily and sent her to a "lockdown" institution in Utah called the Provo Heritage School for Girls. It was a decision my mother now admits may have been a mistake. PHS was a Mormon outfit, replete with surveillance cameras and forlorn inmates who were disallowed forks and knives at mealtimes but permitted to spend hours teasing one another's hair and corrupting one another with outlandish stories of what they'd done to land themselves there. We visited Emily there once, and I came home thoroughly spooked by the image of a tribe of girls in garish makeup and pajamas trotting around the parking circle for exercise under the shadow of the pink and blue Rockies, which stood in a ring around the school like a final, majestic corroboration of their imprisonment.

Emily spent two years at PHS, came home "reformed," enrolled in a local high school, and got a job scooping ice cream. All the while she was making plans to run away with two bad-seed girls she'd hooked up with in Provo. One afternoon about two months later, when Emily was sixteen, they stole my mother's light blue Honda Accord, spray-painted TO HELL OR BUST in black on its side, shaved their heads bald, and hit the road.

First they made a failed, halfhearted attempt to liberate the other girls at PHS, which mostly involved driving around the parking circle, honking in celebration of their freedom. Then they pushed east, hoping to make it as far as the East Village in New York. But they ran out of money in Chicago and had to hole up there for some time, living as skinheads out of my mother's car and on the streets. Eventually a private investigator named "Hal" my mother hired to track them down apprehended them at a Chicago Dunkin' Donuts popular with runaways. "Hal" accompanied them in handcuffs on the plane back to California and delivered them straight to juvenile hall.

While driving to see Emily in juvenile hall at Christmastime, I felt anxious but excited. I hadn't seen her for months, and I had desperately missed our camaraderie, our alliance against our mother's new marriage, our sworn fidelity to our dead father.

There was a lot I didn't miss too. The slammed doors, the covert washing of sex-stained sheets, the *get-away-from-me-you're-not-my-fucking-father* scenes. And while there were certain movies Emily and I both loved and watched obsessively together—*Liquid Sky, Suburbia, Repo Man*—she also had a taste for darker things. For a time she and her friends were into a series of snuff/pseudo-snuff films called *Faces of Death*, which played in the TV room in our shared basement whenever she passed through the house. Just one frame of a *Faces of Death* film was enough to turn my stomach and rot my mind for weeks.

One might think that as fledgling teenagers we would have found ourselves more interested in sex than in death. But we had—or at least Emily had—seemingly exhausted of

54

sex movies, probably from a year or so of unlimited soft-core on Showtime at our father's house. Those movies didn't rot my mind, but they still made me feel guilty and scared. I would crawl to the bottom of Emily's bed while she watched them with friends or babysitters, becoming a small lump under enough covers to ensure that I wouldn't be able to see any of the action or hear any of the cries, even though I knew, or at least suspected, that they were cries of pleasure. It felt important to be there, to be in the room. I guess I didn't want to be alone.

In juvenile hall I first saw Emily behind glass, playing pool with a red bandanna wrapped around her bald head. Her eyes looked bombed-out and vacant. I barely recognized her. After we were buzzed in, she pretended not to see me.

This moment inaugurated a sea change. I came home that night and made my own promise, which I recorded in my diary: I would never care about my sister again. I would never care where she was, if she was lost or found, if she lived or if she died.

I remained grateful, however, for some simple, practical things that she had taught me. How to French-inhale, where to buy bidis, the thin, eucalyptus-leaf cigarettes that I loved, how to draw eyeliner along your inner lids. Emily had told me that all you had to do to get on the pill was complain to a gynecologist that your periods were "irregular," so I did that. I liked my freedom and my anonymity. I had no interest in being shipped away. I got good grades and flew under the radar. Eventually I thought my sister was crazy, or just stupid, to have done so many bad things in plain sight. Even stealing my mother's car seemed too close to home.

Shortly after my sister's release from juvenile hall, my mother and her husband ambushed her again, this time forcibly shipping her off to a "hoods in the woods" school in the deep, Aryan boondocks of Bonner's Ferry, Idaho. Faced with the prospect of chopping wood, solo wilderness-survival expeditions, and an elaborate structure of experimental group and individual therapies with names like "Discovery" and "Summit," Emily quickly split. She made it several miles into the disorienting, frigid forest and encountered the frozen corpse of a horse before she was picked up by the local sheriff and returned to the school, where she stayed for the next two years.

With Emily gone I no longer lay awake at night in my basement room listening to her come and go out her bedroom window. Instead I listened to my mother's husband come and go, either on his motorcycle, or in his painting-company van—a white van with the words FRESH PAINT emblazoned on its side. He played the guitar, although not as well as my father had, and when he was feeling friendly he'd invite me into his "office" to teach me Jimi Hendrix songs. He loved "Red House" in particular.

I never really liked going into his "office," because it was Emily's room, which he had cannibalized in her absence. He had replaced her spiraling collages of rock stars and fashion models with blueprints of houses he was working on and enormous color photographs of a strip of beachfront in Belize that he had purchased with some "business partners." The nature of this business shifted regularly, as did the lineup of partners. He had lived in Belize for a few years in the early '70s with his first wife and his daughter, and now dreamed endlessly of returning there to live off the land. When he felt particularly nostalgic he would pull out his slides from Belize and project them on the wall of the living room. Of these I remember only a group of pale Mennonites who had been his neighbors in the jungle. I knew he kept his machete from those years under his and my mother's bed.

After my stepfather left his "office" at night, I would wander into Emily's dark and abandoned room. I listened to her records. More than once I guiltily jimmied open a desk drawer. Sometimes I found little plastic baggies, empty but cloudy with the residue of white powder. Other drawers yielded stacks of photographs of her mohawked friends flipping the camera the bird. I rifled through the books she had left behind on her bookshelf, many of which I had given her as gifts. I was happy to see that she had dog-eared several pages in Sylvia Plath's *Collected Poems,* which I had given her for her eighth-grade graduation.

That same year, when I was twelve, I submitted a poem to a contest sponsored by our favorite band, The Cure. It was a terrible, melodramatic poem called "Shame." (The band had provided the title; you had to provide the poem to match.) The poem was primarily a collage of Cure lyrics and lines lifted from Plath, and offered an imaginative reconstruction of Emily's experience of losing her virginity.

Miraculously, the poem won the contest. I thought Emily might be furiously jealous, but instead she was incredibly proud, and showed off "Shame" and the letter I received from the band to everyone at school. It was one of the best moments of my life, hands down.

Another book I had lent her was *Rubyfruit Jungle*, the classic lesbian bildungsroman by Rita Mae Brown. Later I reluctantly handed this book over to "Hal" in his search for potential leads in tracking Emily down. I was torn up about it; I knew it was a betrayal. It came from the sycophantic part of me, the part that has always wanted to impress "the adults" with how smart and helpful I could be. It also came from the fact that I was pissed off at her for running away without telling me. It was the first time she hadn't trusted me with a secret, and I wanted to see her punished for it.

But another part of me cheered her on. I wanted her to keep going, to keep pulling one over on our mother and stepfather, to keep saying the big Fuck You to everyone and everything, the big Fuck You I did not say. I wanted her to keep running, to make it, at long last, to wherever it was that she so desperately wanted to go.

MY MOTHER had always told us that Jane had been the rebellious, outspoken daughter, while she had remained the dutiful one. Jane was going to change the world by becoming a fierce civil rights lawyer; my mother was going to get married, put our father through law school by teaching high school English, then stop working and raise two kids. Jane had said all the things to their parents that my mother couldn't or didn't say—the big Fuck You (or, in 1969, *You racist pigs*). As a result, Jane was no longer welcome in their home. If Jane hadn't been estranged from her parents, if she hadn't been worried that they wouldn't accept her decision to marry a leftist Jew and move to New York City, she wouldn't have been coming home alone on March 20, 1969. She wouldn't have advertised for a ride on the ride board, and she wouldn't have ended up with two bullets in her head, stretched out "puffy and lifeless" on a stranger's grave in Denton Cemetery the following morning, her bare ass against the frozen earth, a stranger's stocking buried in her neck.

Dear Jane,

It makes little difference whether it is two nations or two people with conflicting opinions, not much can be done to settle the dispute unless some form of communication is established. It is in this hope that I am writing this letter. I'm sure there is no question in your mind (and in mine) that the contacts we have had in the past year or so have been very disturbing and anything but pleasant. I also recognize the fact that differences in opinion between daughter and parent is a normal situation and fortunately time reduces most of those mountains into mole hills. I'm sure that will be true in our case. But the last few times we have been together have been traumatic emotional experiences

that have accomplished absolutely nothing. I have
no intention of maintaining that kind of
relationship.

So wrote my grandfather on March 4, 1968. But things
between them did not improve—indeed, as Jane's relationship with Phil deepened, and as she elaborated her plan to
elope and move to New York, things worsened. A year later
she was dead. Time did not get its chance to reduce "mountains into mole hills." Instead her death froze these mountains into mountains, and froze her father into a state of
perpetual incomprehension about her, and about their relationship.

RUBYFRUIT JUNGLE turned out to be a helpful lead.
Emily had, in fact, loosely based her travel plans around
Brown's book, which details how one might make money
in the East Village by performing relatively painless sexual
stunts, such as throwing grapefruits at a guy's balls.

DURING THESE years my mother and I went to the
movies together quite often. It was an easy way to spend
time together, sitting in dark places, staring in the same
direction. On weekend days we would drive across the
Golden Gate Bridge into San Francisco, find a good art-
house theater, pay one round of admission, and then sneak
from film to film: her trick. But a problem recurred—she

couldn't tolerate scenes that involved the abduction of women, especially into cars, and she couldn't watch women be threatened with guns, especially guns pointed at their heads.

Try going to the movies with this rule, and you will be surprised at how often such scenes crop up.

I left home at seventeen, for college, and for New York, where I soon discovered the deep pleasure of going to the movies by myself. Yet whenever such a scene arose I immediately felt my mother close beside me in the dark theater. Her hands spread across her face, her pinkies pushing down on her eyelids so she can't see, her index fingers pushing down on her ears so she can't hear.

I felt her this way acutely when I went to see *Taxi Driver* at the Film Forum in Greenwich Village several years ago. I was excited—it was the first screening of a new print, and a classic I'd never seen. Waiting in line my excitement dampened a little upon noticing that I was one of the only women, and certainly one of the only solo women, at the theater. The crowd was solid boy film geeks, probably NYU film students, who had apparently come prepared to treat the screening like a performance of *The Rocky Horror Picture Show,* screaming out in chorus the movie's many famous lines seconds before the characters spoke them. This was tolerable, sometimes even amusing, until a passenger in Travis Bickle's taxicab embarked upon the following monologue, which the passenger—played by Scorsese himself—delivers while watching his wife through the window of another man's house:

I'm gonna kill her. I'm gonna kill her with a .44 Magnum pistol. I have a .44 Magnum pistol. I'm gonna kill her with that gun. Did you ever see what a .44 Magnum pistol can do to a woman's face? I mean it'll fuckin' destroy it. Just blow her right apart. That's what it can do to her face. Now, did you ever see what it can do to a woman's pussy? That you should see. You should see what a .44 Magnum's gonna do to a woman's pussy you should see.

Sitting alone in a sea of young men hollering, *Did you ever see what a .44 can do to a woman's pussy?* was not amusing. Perhaps it was not tolerable, or perhaps I should not have tolerated it. I sat through the rest of the movie, but as I walked slowly home down the dark cobblestone streets of Soho toward my apartment on Orchard Street I found myself thinking about my mother, and about Jane, and about Emily, with tears streaming down my cheeks. *That you should see.*

ON ONE VISIT back to San Francisco in 1996, my mother and I returned to one of our old haunts, the Opera Plaza Cinema on Van Ness, to see a movie we knew virtually nothing about, save that it was a "dark comedy" titled *Freeway.* In its opening scenes a wayward teen played by Reese Witherspoon steals a car and runs away from her truly screwed-up family. Her car then breaks down on a California freeway, and a seemingly well-meaning yuppie, played by Kiefer Sutherland, pulls over to help. In his car they have a wide-ranging conversation, which takes a turn for the worse when he starts talking about wanting to rape her dead body. She then realizes that he is the so-called "I-5 Killer," and he intends to make her his next victim.

By this point in the movie—just about ten minutes in— I could see that we were going to have to pack up. But as we started to gather our things, the movie took another turn. Witherspoon gains control of the situation by pulling out her boyfriend's gun. She asks Sutherland if he believes that Jesus Christ is his personal savior, then shoots him in the neck several times. Then she throws up, steals his car, and leaves him for dead on the side of the road.

I don't think he actually dies, but to be honest I remember little to nothing about the rest. What I remember is the moment in the small dark theater, right before Witherspoon pulls out her gun, right before we stood up to leave, when my mother leaned over and whispered to me, *Let's give it one more minute—maybe something different is about to happen.*

American Taboo

THE FIRST E-MAIL I receive from *48 Hours Mystery* comes a few months before the trial from a producer who addresses me as "Mrs. Nelson," unwittingly conjuring up an identity held but fleetingly by my mother many years ago. In his e-mail the producer says that he hopes I will consider working with them, as he feels strongly that "my family's story of struggle and hope" has great relevance to their audience.

I ponder this phrase for some time. I wonder if he is imagining my family as the kind to print up T-shirts with Jane's picture and a "we will never forget" slogan on them, as I have seen some families on these TV shows do. I wonder if he read the article in the *Detroit Free Press* in December 2004 in which my grandfather likened the reopening of Jane's case to "picking a scab." I wonder what he would think if he knew that after the January hearing, when Hiller asked my grandfather what he thought of the court proceedings thus far, my grandfather said he found them "boring."

I agree to meet the producer for dinner at a restaurant on the Upper West Side of Manhattan.

• • •

THE NIGHT before we meet I stay up late perusing the Web site for *48 Hours Mystery*. I learn that *48 Hours* used to focus on "human interest" stories of varying degrees of social importance—the international sex trade, the pros and cons of the "Subway Diet," the risks of gastric bypass surgery. But as ratings for investigative journalism plummeted and ratings for true-crime shows began to soar, "*48 Hours*" became "*48 Hours Mystery*." At times they attempt to take on deeper topics within the "murder mystery" rubric—a recent show, for example, investigates the topic *Who Killed Jesus?* and stars Elaine Pagels.

As I scroll down the long list of show titles I feel my spirits start to sink. There are a host of stories about missing or murdered girls and women, with panic-inducing titles like *Where's Baby Sabrina? Where's Molly? Where Is Mrs. March?* Others feature high-profile cases—*JonBenét: DNA Rules Out Parents; Is Amber Still in Love with Scott?: Her Father Says She Has Never Gotten Over Him*, while others strive for a more poetic effect: *Dark Side of the Mesa: Did Michael Blagg Murder His Wife and Daughter?* I try to imagine the title they'll choose for Jane's show but come up dry.

I FIND the producer on a street corner on Broadway, talking outside the restaurant with some of his college friends, all of whom graduated just a couple of years ago. I'm surprised—I had imagined dinner with a slick patrician, a hard-boiled veteran of the TV business. The surprise is apparently mutual: when we sit down, he tells me that I look way too young to be a professor, and he's taken aback that I'm not married. I have no idea why he thought I was.

We are meeting early in the evening because he has to fly to Los Angeles first thing in the morning to cover the Michael Jackson child molestation trial. I am not very interested in the Jackson trial, but I try to make small talk about other famous trials. I bring up Gary Gilmore and Norman Mailer's *The Executioner's Song*; he says he hasn't heard of Norman Mailer, but will definitely look him up. He orders us a bottle of Sauvignon Blanc, and appears perplexed when it arrives. *I thought I ordered us a red,* he says, decanting with a shrug.

Over the wine he asks me if, while writing *Jane,* I felt as though I were channeling my aunt. I say no. He looks disappointed. I try to explain that *Jane* is about identification, not fusion. That I never even knew her. That in the book I don't try to speak for her, but rather to let her speak for herself, through her journal entries. And that although I have tried to imagine her death, there's really no way of knowing what she went through—not only because I don't know what happened to her on the night of her murder, but because no one ever really knows what it's like to be in anyone else's skin. That no living person can tell another what it's like to die. That we do that part alone.

Our entrees arrive—stylish piles of monkfish—and he shifts gears, says it's time for the "hard sell." He says that although *48 Hours Mystery* strives to entertain, it always keeps a serious social issue at stake. When I ask him what the issue might be in this case, he says this episode will be about grief. About helping other people to mourn. He says that my family's involvement could really help other people in similar situations.

All those viewers who thought they lost a family member to a famous serial killer, then are told 36 years later that DNA from the crime scene matches both that of a retired nurse and a man who was four years old at the time and grew up to murder his mother, I think.

With less graciousness than I'd hoped to display, I ask if there's a reason why stories about the bizarre, violent deaths of young, good-looking, middle- to upper-class white girls help people to mourn better than other stories.

I thought it might come to this, he says good-naturedly but warily, refolding the napkin in his lap.

After dinner we walk a few blocks up Broadway together and pass one of the gigantic, brightly lit Barnes & Nobles that now sprawl around so many New York City street corners. He lights up with an idea—he says he's going in to find the Mailer book I told him about, which he will read on the plane to California tomorrow morning. *Good idea,* I say, not mentioning that it's 1,056 pages. He beckons me into the store, says he'll buy me anything I want, on his CBS account.

I know I should decline. But a wicked you're-using-me-so-why-shouldn't-I-use-you feeling has already taken root.

We browse for a bit on our own, then reconvene at the cash register. I have James Ellroy's 1996 "crime memoir," *My Dark Places,* in my hand.

My Dark Places is a sinister, engrossing book about the 1958 murder of Ellroy's mother and his subsequent sexual and literary obsession with vivisected women. I had furtively skimmed this book in various bookstores while working on *Jane* over the past few years, but had always felt too ashamed to buy it for myself. It seems the perfect memento for this evening.

In parting the producer hands me a sample videotape of his show, which I deposit into my plastic Barnes & Noble shopping bag.

I take the train back to Connecticut the next morning and stuff the shopping bag under my dresser as if trying to forget a one-night stand I'd prefer never happened. The bag sits there for over a month. When I finally pull it out, I stack the book and videotape on top of each other on my desk in the Ponderosa Room, where they sit untouched for several more weeks.

The label on the videotape reads: *American Taboo: Who Murdered a Beautiful Peace Corps Volunteer in Tonga?*

At long last, one night I pull my TV out of the closet, curl up on the couch, and insert *American Taboo* into the VCR.

The show opens with a photo of a truly gorgeous brunette chewing playfully, erotically, on a long piece of grass. Then a true-crime writer who has written a book about this woman, whose name was Deborah Gardner, appears against a mountainous backdrop, and explains why he became obsessed with her. He says it had something to do with the combination of her beauty and the horror of her 1976 murder. He then quotes Edgar Allan Poe, who once declared the death of a beautiful woman to be the most poetic topic in the world.

I'm taken aback: I used this same Poe quotation in *Jane*.

The show then vacillates between more lovely photos of Gardner and photos of her blood-splattered hut in Tonga, where a fellow Peace Corps volunteer stabbed her twenty-two times. (He is later found not guilty by reason of insanity in a Tonga court.) The camera whirls around her hut in a restaging of her murder, first from the perspective of her deranged killer, then from that of a panicked, dying Gardner, fighting hopelessly for her life. There are several stills of the long, serrated hunting knife apparently used to do the deed.

I can't make it to the end of *American Taboo*. I try on a few other occasions, but every time I end up symptomatically falling asleep, or shutting it off in despair.

THE SHOW about Jane, which will air on Thanksgiving weekend, 2005, will be titled *Deadly Ride*. I won't watch it either, even though my mother and I will ostensibly be its stars. People will assure me that we brought some dignity, some depth to the genre, and to Jane's life, and I will be glad. That was the point of participating, as they were going to do the show with or without us. But I don't want to see the crime scene photos flashed over and over again on TV, nor do I want to think about millions of Americans flipping by Jane's corpse under its bloodstained raincoat while channel-surfing at their in-laws, up late, still stuffed from Thanksgiving dinner.

IT TAKES ME even longer to crack the Ellroy memoir, but I manage to finish it in one sitting. As with *American Taboo*, there are some discomfiting parallels.

Ellroy's mother died when he was ten. Exactly thirty-six years later he decides to research and write about her long-repressed murder. Eventually he is able to reopen her case, which he works on with a homicide cop from the LAPD.

Ellroy also suffers from murder mind, but his turns him on. The titular "dark place"—the fantasy that nearly drives him to insanity—is that of fucking his mutilated mother. *Her amputated nipple thrills me.*

Despite all his hard work on the case, Ellroy's mother's murder remains unsolved; at the end of the book he provides a contact number for tips. *I'll learn more,* he promises his dead mother on the last page. *You're gone and I want more of you.*

It's a disappointing ending. Not because the case doesn't get solved, but because Ellroy never seems to grasp the futility of his enterprise. Instead his compulsion to "learn more" just smashes up against this futility with increasing velocity. He knows that no amount of information about his mother's life or death will bring her back, but somehow he doesn't really seem to get it.

I don't get it either.

I've never had the desire or need to bring Jane back—I

never even knew her. And while the unsolved status of her murder may have once haunted me, now a man has been arrested for it, is being held without bail, and will soon be brought to trial. And yet, daily, while in faculty meetings or paused at traffic lights, I find myself scrawling lists of potential avenues of further inquiry. Should I visit Leiterman in prison? Interview members of his family? Find Johnny Ruelas? Spend more time with Schroeder? What on earth for?

Conventional wisdom has it that we dredge up family stories to find out more about ourselves, to pursue that all-important goal of "self-knowledge," to catapult ourselves, like Oedipus, down the track that leads to the revelation of some original crime, some original truth. Then we gouge our eyes out in shame, run screaming into the wilderness, and plagues cease to rain down upon our people.

Fewer people talk about what happens when this track begins to dissolve, when the path starts to become indistinguishable from the forest.

Photo #3:

A close-up of the entry wound in Jane's lower left skull. Her hair, thick and red with blood, has been pushed aside to expose it, as if to isolate a tick in the fur of an animal. Around the hole is a bright-red corona of flayed skin which the examiner calls a "contusion collar." The diameter of the wound is very small; a .22 is not a big-caliber gun.

A speck of white light from the medical examiner's laser pen dances in and around the wound for almost twenty min-

utes. At first I think the puckered hole looks like a sea urchin. Then I think it looks like an anus. The lingering close-up makes me feel like doing something perverse—I feel like standing up and starting to sing. I imagine the courtroom suddenly sliding over into musical farce, a self-help spoof I would title "Circling the Wound."

Murder Mind, Redux

THROUGHOUT THE winter of 2004–2005 the biggest local story in Middletown, Connecticut, was the impending execution of convicted serial killer Michael Ross. The execution was scheduled to take place a few towns away, and was to be the first execution in New England since 1960.

Ross's killing spree bore many similarities to the Michigan Murders. He started out in 1981 on the campus of Cornell University, and over the next three years killed eight girls and young women; John Collins had been a student at Eastern Michigan University, and many of the girls he allegedly killed were students at either Eastern or the U of M. Unlike Collins, however, who to this day maintains his innocence from prison, Ross pled guilty. Also unlike Collins, Ross was convicted in a state with the death penalty, and in 1987 Ross was sentenced to death by lethal injection.

Over the next eighteen years on death row Ross filed a variety of appeals—to be castrated, to be retried, to be executed. But as his execution date in January 2005 drew near he refused to file any more. In court after court he and his lawyer insisted that he was mentally competent, that he knew what he was doing. Like Gary Gilmore before him, Ross was fighting to die. *I want no gravestone, no reminders . . . I just want to be forgotten,* he said in an interview posted on the elaborate Web site he maintained from prison.

On this same Web site, Ross described his mental state—which is clinically (if broadly) classified as "sexual sadism"—as follows:

> I guess the easiest way to explain it is everybody's had a tune in their head, like a melody that they heard on the radio or something. It just plays over and over again . . . I have that & no matter how hard you try to get rid of that melody, it's still there. And that kind of thing could drive you nuts. But if you replace that melody now with thoughts of rape & murder & degradation of women . . .

This description chilled me to the bone. It was an excellent description of murder mind.

On January 23, 2005—the Sunday before his Wednesday execution date—the *Hartford Courant* was thick with Ross. I saw its front page through a cracked, graffitied newspaper box on Main Street, in front of a Dunkin' Donuts that served as a kind of halfway house for the town's many vagrants. The Dunkin' Donuts was adjacent to the local theater, which was now featuring the horror movie *Saw.* Its poster featured a woman's severed, bloody leg, alongside the tagline *How much blood would you shed to stay alive?*

I went inside to get change, bought the edition with a fistful of quarters, and sat down at the counter to look at it.

The front page bore several large color photographs of four girls and young women, with this text underneath them:

These [victims] were snatched by a man who first made small talk with them, then forced them into his car or into the woods. He has admitted to raping all but one. After the rapes he forced them to roll over on their stomachs. Then he would straddle them and strangle them from behind.

I knew these kinds of articles well. A few years back I had spent a long, sweltering summer printing out dozens of them from microfilm in the basement of the New York Public Library in service of *Jane*. I blasted through reel after reel of the *Detroit News*, keeping my eyes peeled for the row of photographs that signified the dead girls. Invariably I would get moored up in the wedding pages until I realized my error: *Not dead, just married.*

Although over thirty years apart, the *Detroit News* and *Hartford Courant* articles kept to a similar script. They both paired a "she had so much to live for" sentimentality with quasi-pornographic descriptions of the violence each girl had suffered. The main difference was that the '60s articles used a more modest lexicon: "violated," "co-ed," etc.–and that they were sandwiched in between articles about the war in Vietnam instead of the war in Iraq.

How does one measure the loss of eight young women? asked the *Courant. There is no way to know what they would have done with their lives—the careers they might have pursued, the people they would have loved, the children they might have had.*

I know that I am supposed to care about these questions. Especially as the author of *Jane,* in which I bent over backwards to pay more attention to Jane's life than to her death. But somehow they instantaneously make me *not* want to read on. How does one measure the loss of anyone? Is measurement a necessary part of grief? Is a life less grievable if its prospects for the future—here imagined as a range of career options and the potential to bear children—*don't* appear bright? *The people they would have loved*—that was a nice touch. But what about the people they already had loved? Or what if they hadn't loved anyone, or no one had loved them?

More to the point, I knew that this tally of grief, along with the brutal physical details of Ross's rapes and murders, was supposed to do more than bring tears to one's eyes or sell papers. It was also supposed to drum up support for the long-dormant death penalty in Connecticut, and in New England at large. The "Commentary" section regularly rehashed the most heinous aspects of Ross's crimes before immediately reminding the reader, *The vast majority of people in this state and country continue to support the death penalty for certain types of murders—*i.e., for *this* kind.

So despite the fact that the so-called "Blizzard of '05" had just dumped two feet of snow in the Connecticut region, in addition to bringing subzero temperatures and wind gusts of hurricane proportions, I was planning to attend the overnight protest march and vigil at the Osborn Correctional Institution in Somers, Connecticut, where Ross was to be executed in the dead of night.

The principal organizers of the protest set up a helpful if daunting informational Web site that listed all the ways one might protect against or treat hypothermia. One steadfast, activist colleague of mine at the university promised to go with me no matter what; another begged me not to go, insisting that my presence wouldn't affect what happened, and all I would do out there was freeze to death. I tried to explain to her that you don't go to a vigil expecting to halt an action. You go to bear witness to what the state would prefer to do in complete darkness. And if your family has lost a loved one via an act of violence, you speak out so that advocates of capital punishment can't keep relying on the anger and grief of victims' families as grounds for their agenda. I tell her that I consider antiviolence activists to be bodhisattvas, "master warriors"—*not warriors who kill and harm but warriors of nonaggression who hear the cries of the world,* as one Buddhist book puts it. *[M]en and women who are willing to train in the middle of the fire . . . [men and women who] enter challenging situations in order to alleviate suffering.*

The author of an essay with the frightening title "The Moral Worth of Retribution," which I came across in a primer called *What Is Justice?* lent to me by an ethicist at the university, sees things differently:

My own view is that [a transfer of concern from victim to criminal] occurs in large part because of our unwillingness to face our own revulsion at what was done. It allows us to look away from the horror that another person was willing to cause. We almost cannot bear the sight. . . . By repressing anger at wrongful violation, we may be attempting to deny that we live in a society in which there really are fearful and awful people.

Certainly I didn't feel unwilling to face my revulsion. Sometimes I felt as though that was all I was doing. But was I "repressing anger at wrongful violation"? Was I denying the fact that "we live in a society in which there really are fearful and awful people"? What would it mean *not* to deny such a thing?

Ross's execution didn't happen that winter. A federal judge threatened to disbar Ross's lawyer for being insufficiently suspicious of his client's willingness to die, and the lawyer subsequently requested a new hearing on Ross's competency. The execution was delayed indefinitely.

To Hell or Bust

THE LONG, dismal winter in Middletown finally gave way to spring, and my mother and I both found ourselves on the fence about whether or not to attend Leiterman's summer trial in full. It would be expensive, it would require canceling weeks of work, it was more or less guaranteed to be traumatic in ways that were impossible to foresee. The state had offered to put us up in a single room in a motel, and the idea of sharing a motel room with my mother for a month during a murder trial sounded like a setting for a macabre reality TV show. Worse, I flashed momentarily upon the ghastly scene in the French film *The Piano Teacher* in which Isabelle Huppert, who sleeps nightly with her mother in the same bed, suddenly attacks her in such a way that you can't tell if she's trying to rape her or kill her or both.

But this notion of bearing witness—of trying to approximate these noble warrior-bodhisattvas heading into the fire—had a hold on me. Jane's mother, my grandmother, had died many years ago, and neither Jane's father nor brother wanted to go to court every day. Emily, who had by now rejoined the fold and moved back to the Bay Area, wanted to come but couldn't get off work. It became clear that if my mother and I didn't go, the front-row bench reserved for Jane's family would sit empty. That seemed plainly wrong.

So we committed to attending together. She'd fly in from California, and I'd drive my car from Connecticut so that we won't have to pay for a rental car. Eventually her cousin Jill, who lives within walking distance of the courthouse, will graciously offer to stay with her boyfriend for the month, giving us her house so that we won't have to stay at a motel. Emily says she will try to fly in for the verdict.

On 6 A.M. on the morning of July 10, 2005, on the eve of jury selection, as I was getting in the car to drive the twelve hours from Middletown to Michigan, however, the plan seemed wrong. Simply put, in the meantime, I had become a brokenheart. As winter moved into spring, then spring into summer, I found myself losing the man I loved. I was falling, or had fallen, out of a story, the story of a love I wanted very much. Too much, probably. And the pain of the loss had deranged me.

Falling out of a story hurts. But it's nothing compared to the loss of an actual person, the loss of all the bright details that make up that person. All the flashing, radiant fragments that constitute an affair, or a love. If there has been a betrayal, you may find yourself holding each of these fragments up to a new light and rotating them there, watching each one grow an unwanted shadow. I found myself there.

In May I had been on a book tour for *Jane* throughout

the South, and had returned to the East Coast excited to
see him. When he didn't answer my calls, I wondered if I'd
misunderstood something about his work schedule, which
was incredibly hectic and far-flung. In a fit of uneasiness
laced with foreboding and shame, I punched his name and
the date into Google. I hated myself for doing so even
before I clicked "Search."

Up came a blog, right off the bat, which reported having just seen this person at an event with his girlfriend,
who was, apparently, a movie star. *She's much smaller and
more beautiful in person,* raved the blogger. *And very down-to-
earth.*

This was news to me. It was not news, however, to anyone in cyberspace, not to mention in the "real" world.
Soon I would find out that it wasn't even news to some of
my best friends.

I HAD MET this man two years earlier, exactly nine days
after my boyfriend of many years and I had moved into
our first apartment together. I had never lived with anyone
before, and I felt intense trepidation—so much so that as
we began our move I became convinced that the leaky loft
we were about to co-inhabit was full of a toxic dust that
would kill me. This wasn't complete madness—the loft was
perched on the Gowanus Canal in Brooklyn, a notoriously
polluted waterway that purportedly carries live strains of
hepatitis. The loft was industrial, not legally zoned for living, with a stall of oil trucks next door that steadily belched

up a dense black soot, which within a week of unpacking had coated all my books and dishes. Upon moving in my boyfriend's cat developed multiple cysts and hid atop a cupboard; mine yowled all night and peed incessantly on my boyfriend's most treasured belongings. Both of us quickly developed a pulmonary affliction we called "the canal cough," which manifested itself whenever the wind shifted direction and brought particles from the nearby cement factory our way. It was deadly quiet at night; if there was any sound at all you knew it was trouble. The Gowanus is the end of the line, and has been for over a century—home to prostitutes and johns who seem to crawl out of its weird banks like moss-people, and an infamous spot for dumping bodies, garbage, and cars. Policemen laugh if a suspect they are chasing jumps into the canal to get away—they know he'll end up in the hospital, sick from the water, within days.

I lasted forty-one days in this loft, like Noah. My departure was cruel, my boyfriend said. More than cruel: sadistic. I agreed, but I didn't feel as though I had a choice. I had fallen precipitously in love with this other man, the kind of love that makes whatever you'd been doing before feel instantly untenable. The kind that comes on like a derailed train—all you can do is stand back and wait for it to crash, then stagger around in the wreckage, too dazed yet to wonder who to blame, what the cause.

On my last night in the Gowanus loft my boyfriend asked if he could choke me with a silk stocking while we fucked. I assented; I even got the stocking out of my drawer myself. I have always had an erotic fondness for asphyxiation. It feels good not to breathe a short while before coming, so that when you finally come and breathe together, you get an astonishing rush: the world comes back to you in a flood of color, pleasure, and breath.

I did not know that earlier that day he had read my journal, and had there found out that I was in love with someone else, that I had made love with someone else. I had only told him that I was leaving. As we had sex I suddenly suspected that he knew more than I'd told him. I suspected this when I said, aghast, *This is how Jane died,* and he said, without missing a beat, *I know.*

Years before, I had had a lover who was a welder. As a gift he once welded me the single most beautiful object that I own. It is a palm-sized box made of Plexiglas, with several stacked layers of blue-greenish broken glass sealed inside. The box, he explained to me, is the love. It is the container that can hold all the brokenness, and make it beautiful. Especially when you hold it up to the light.

This is what I wanted love to be.

I wish I could say I left the loft for the man I'd fallen in love with—and I would have, but that was not our story. But I had hope, a dogged, superstitious hope that sustained our affair for the next two years. Until the blog about the movie star.

But if I were honest, or if I were at least to bump into the limits of my honesty, I would have to admit that I knew exactly how this love would end from the moment it began. The loss was probable before it was possible.

Maybe it was even actual before it was possible. Why else was I punching his name through Google, becoming someone I despised? The end of the story was clear from the start. I just didn't care. People in love rarely do. And like most people in love, or maybe like most writers in love, I thought if I could keep formulating it correctly, if I could keep finding the right words to house it, maybe I could change it.

But, of course, I was not its sole author.

A FEW DAYS before I leave for the trial I go visit a friend and his wife on Cape Cod, hoping to start eating, feel human, get my act together. I spend the entire visit weeping uncontrollably. On the fourth night of hearing me sob in their guest room, my friend's wife takes pity on me, tiptoes into my room, and silently hands me a fistful of Ambien. After I nearly faint on the beach the following day my friend says to me in exasperation, *You can't live on cigarettes and agony alone, you know.*

I am getting the bad feeling that my friends are growing tired of me. I am growing tired of me, too.

I am also becoming painfully aware of the fact that I am not and have never been a "master warrior." Not even close. Instead of hoping to alleviate some of my mother's suffering at the trial, train in the middle of the fire, or bear any noble kind of witness for Jane, now I'm just hoping to stay alive.

For at some point during this time the coin flipped.

The zoo of murder mind slipped into the zoo of suicide mind. I watched it happen as though it were happening to the mind of another.

Stay curious, the Buddhists advise. I tried.

I watched my suicide mind with interest as well as panic, trying to think of it as a jerky slide show, a scary movie playing behind my eyes, one I could keep watching or walk out of at any time. (*Into where,* I can't say.)

The only person with whom I had ever discussed suicide mind at length was my junkie boyfriend, years ago. Or, rather, we discussed his suicide mind, which most closely resembled, so far as I could tell, a diorama. His ideations always involved a tableau of sorts, a scene happened upon by another. The door swings open, the mouth falls agape, a ripple of shock charges through the air, a fresh wave of damage breaks—not a coda but a reprise, a skip in the groove, a scratch that will not mend no matter how many times the record is played. *The song remains the same.* The two scenes that recurred for him most often were that of his body hanging from a cord in the center of his bedroom in his Victorian squat in Staten Island, snow from the harbor blowing in through the open windows, and that of his body slumped over on his desk after an overdose, his "works" beside him—which would include his great unfinished novel, *Goiter,* a Joycean, barely fictionalized account of his mother's madness, and of her goiter, both of which, from what I had personally observed, were nothing short of ghastly.

These tableaux held no appeal for me. They seemed to

depend upon a traumatized observer, a dependence that seemed to me weak, sadistic. Narcissistic in its theatricality, and a bit silly, all things considered.

My suicide mind contained, or contains, no before and no after, no swung-open doors, no pain done unto others and none, paradoxically, done unto myself. Just one single gesture—one implacable, irreversible action that cleaves my body (cleanly, simply) out of time and mind.

AS I GOT ready to leave for the trial I sometimes felt as though the pain of this loss was delivering me unto a form of enlightenment—that through it I was finally coming to grasp that our thoughts, our emotions, our entire lives, are essentially an illusion, a long, rich, various dream from which our death wakes us.

Whosoever shall seek to save his life shall lose it; and whosoever shall lose his life shall preserve it. Another red part.

This line of thinking seemed preferable to the other option: that I was slipping into a disassociated, heartbroken fog that any number of contemporary Western psychiatrists would rush to medicate.

Cure only comes if the patient reaches to the original state of breakdown, Winnicott wrote. Reaches *to,* not reaches: a crucial distinction. I have no idea how anyone makes it.

What I do know is this (and here I speak, of course, only for myself): there is no saving thought (*think how your _____ will feel; count your blessings; tomorrow is another day;* etc.) that is ultimately sustaining, no line of poetry, no holy book, no hotline, nothing but the thinnest of membranes, *a doctrine whispered in secret, that man is a prisoner who has no right to open the door and run away.*

This is a great mystery which I do not quite understand, Socrates says of this doctrine, shortly before he drinks the cup of hemlock that will cause his death—a death which, two thousand years after the fact, scholars are still debating whether can or should be termed a suicide.

FOR THE MONTH that I am in Ann Arbor, I will write letters to the man I loved on my yellow legal pad every morning before my mother wakes up, letters telling him how much I miss him, how much my body misses him. I will tell him all about the trial, to which he had said he would accompany me. I will describe each of the autopsy photos in detail, convinced that only he can understand their burden, their horror. I won't send any of these letters. Even though I have told him that I never want to hear from him again as long as I live, I will check my e-mail on Jill's computer every night, in case he has written.

He does write, once. He says that our separation has brought him no joy, but that he feels it's an important part of the journey, the journey of "stepping into the light." I have no idea what journey, what light, he's talking about. I have never felt so lost, never felt such darkness. Perhaps he is talking about his journey, his light. I am coming to see that we no longer share either.

Every morning before court and every night after I will

take a long shower, as the shower is the only place I will have any privacy. In the stall I will get down on my knees and weep, letting the water run over my body, praying to get better, praying not to hurt myself any more than I'm already hurting, praying that this loss, that this whole time, will move over me, through me, like a dark storm passing over a great plain. A great plain which is, essentially, my soul. A soul which is neither light nor dark, neither wholly alone nor wholly with any other, certainly not with God, just flat, open, deathless, and free. Curled up in a wet ball on the tile floor I will hear myself say, *Something in me is dying.* I no longer know to whom I'm talking.

Photo #4:

Jane again on the gurney, its metallic shine underneath her neck and face. A head-on shot, from the sternum upwards, a red ruler under her chin, as if for scale. As if she were an improbable dwarf or visitor from a differently sized planet, instead of a dead woman on a gurney. Her features look jumbled—put together more as a jigsaw puzzle than a face, the red ruler beneath her chin a vain effort to organize her flesh. Her eyes are closed, and the area above them, from eyelid to eyebrow, is bright blue. It looks like heavy eyeshadow, but the examiner explains that the blue is blood that has collected behind the skin. The color is so intense because the skin at that site on our bodies is about as thin as a Kleenex.

Apart from the weird blue sheen, the clotted blood, and the red ruler, here Jane looks just like my mother. Specifically, her nostrils look just like my mother's—the same two, slim water-

melon seeds. This could have been my mother's fate, as she feared for years it might be. It could be anybody's.

Once I wondered how they knew that Jane was shot before she was strangled. Now I know. It has to do with two different kinds of blue. If she had died from asphyxiation, her whole face would have a bluish color, a color the examiner terms "unmistakable." But the only blue here is the blue blood above her eyes. If she had been strangled first, the stocking would have acted as a tourniquet, and this blood would not have been able to move up to her face. The examiner explains that the force of the bullets fired into Jane's skull fractured her orbital bones—the bony cavities that contain our eyes—and the blue is all the blood that rushed around the injury.

This photo may be the worst of them all, I'm not sure. It all depends on what one means by worst. It shows that the body hurries to heal itself, even as it's dying.

Sybaris

My MOTHER AND I had convinced each other before meeting up in Michigan that our time in Ann Arbor might be a kind of respite. She imagined a month off work, lots of time to think and read, early morning walks, cooking quiet dinners, maybe even trying her hand, at long last, at one of the writing projects she'd always dreamed of undertaking. I imagined a month of getting some distance, or at least distraction, from my heartache, finding a local pool to swim laps in, and quitting smoking, especially so as not to face my mother's censure.

After the first day of jury selection, we realize our mutual folly. Every day after court we will stumble home down Main Street feeling as though we've been whacked with a slab of wood. Every night will be too hot to cook or sleep. We have to leave for court each morning by seven and we don't get home until after six, so we are together almost constantly. "Taking space" from each other means walking to or from the courthouse staggered apart by a block, or going to sleep.

LET ME EXPLAIN, says the very first potential juror questioned at the voir dire. He's Italian, about sixty, tan, wearing Birkenstocks, bald except for a squirrelly pony-tail. *I am an artist. I have the heart, the soul, of an artist. That means that in my world, there are no criminals. In my world, there are no crimes. In my world*—he closes his eyes beatifically, gesturing out to an imaginary plain—*everything is beautiful.*

The judge looks exasperated. *If chosen for this jury, can you agree to live in* this *world, with the rest of us, right now?*

The artist shakes his head. *I'm sorry, but I cannot. I cannot live in your world.*

INSTEAD OF quitting smoking, I find that my mother wants to smoke with me. She complains that my cigarettes are too strong, however, so I start buying ultra-lights for her, and breaking off their filters for me. If I'm going to smoke, I'm not going to try to suck blood from a stone.

FOR A PORTION of this time there's a summer street fair set up along Main Street, the Ann Arbor Arts Festival. My mother and I had heard about this fair before coming, and thought it might provide some relief, even some plea-sure. Now getting spit out of the grim courthouse each evening into a bustling, cheerful mecca of corndog stands, bad landscape paintings, and glazed pottery makes us feel trapped in a Fellini movie.

• • •

Sybaris

AT THE VOIR dire the judge asks all the potential jurors to swear that even if they regularly watch *CSI*, *Law & Order*, *Cold Case Files*, or any other television show featuring forensic science and criminal justice, that they have a firm grasp on the difference between television—even reality television—and reality itself, in which we are presumably now mired. One potential juror with several small children says that won't be a problem for her, because she mostly watches the Cartoon Network; the judge quips that an afternoon spent with the Cartoon Network provides as much or more information about the criminal justice system as a full season of *Law & Order*.

One by one, each juror solemnly swears to his or her capacity to distinguish between dramatization and reality, between fact and fiction. This strikes me as completely disingenuous. But then again, who's going to sit there in the jury box and say, *Actually, Your Honor, I admit it. I can't tell the difference between representation and reality anymore. I'm very sorry.*

FOR THE FIRST three days of trial my mother and I arrive at the courthouse to find ourselves adrift in a sea of heavy-set, elderly men. Retired cops, detectives, ambulance drivers, and medical examiners waiting to testify in our case jam the corridors, ambling about on their canes, greeting each other with slaps on the back as if it's a high school reunion. All of their bodies emanate a faded, patrician majesty, and seem stuffed into their civilian suits. Several of their faces drag with strokes. Many have slurred speech, and are either going deaf or are already there.

I really can't hear a word you're saying, sighs the now-ancient morgue wagon driver who transported Jane's body on the afternoon of March 21, 1969. *All I know is that I came to the scene like I always did, and I loaded her up.*

Three days solid, eight hours a day, dozens of witnesses, no women. Just two male attorneys, the male judge, the male defendant, a coterie of male detectives, and a parade of male retirees recalling their interaction with Jane's dead body, pictures of which they draw upon from the witness box with little laser pens. Nancy Grow is resubpoenaed, but she never reappears. Her doctor has submitted a note saying that the stress of testifying again on this matter would be mortally dangerous to her health. In her place Hiller shows the jury a digital recording of her January testimony. The quality of the footage is bad—Grow flickers in and out, looking even more distressed than she had in person. More disconcerting still is the appearance of my family on this recording, as we all come into view whenever the camera pans over to our bench. We look awful—washed-out, shocked, teary—a mirror image of ourselves today, except that now the cast of characters has thinned out, and we are no longer dressed for winter.

And so Grow tells her story again. The same blood-stained bag, the same *Maybe it's a dummy,* the same loafers and nightgown, the same screaming, the same shame, this time her grainy, sepia figure looking very much like the hologram of Princess Leia in *Star Wars* as she repeatedly appeals, *Help me Obi-Won Kenobi, you're my only hope.*

AS A RULE, my mother does not sleep well. After I go to bed at Jill's I hear her fluttering around the house like a ghost. On good nights she talks excitedly to her new boyfriend on her cell phone; on bad nights she drinks wine until it's gone, then rummages around for something else, anything else. Sits in the dark kitchen, drinking Kahlúa.

But compared to my state, and compared to where she's been, she is doing quite well. A couple of years ago, after a little over twenty years of marriage, her husband, the housepainter, left abruptly and cruelly. His departure, along with the messy divorce proceedings that ensued, plunged her headlong into loneliness and despair. Her anxiety about being alone for the first time in her life was acute: she could barely go to the grocery store, for example, because she thought strangers were pitying her for buying single servings of food.

I tried to help at the beginning of this period, flying out to California to meet with her and her divorce lawyer, cleaning out my stepfather's belongings from spaces that were too painful for her to enter. But one afternoon, while scrubbing down his walk-in closet with disinfectant at her request, I lost it. We had been here before. Twenty years earlier my mother and I had spent an afternoon together cleaning out my father's closet a few weeks after his death, getting his house ready to sell. The same cardboard boxes, the same cylinder of Ajax. The same muted mania in the face of abandonment. *Just us chickens.*

I had gone along then because I suspected there might be things of my father's I wanted to keep, and there were. I also wanted to seem brave. More than that, I wanted to *be* brave, though I didn't have a clue what that might entail. But my stepfather hadn't died, he'd just split without saying good-bye, and I didn't want to pay him the kindness of dealing with his stuff. Certainly I didn't want any of it.

The more needy my mother became, the less I could help her. Her habitual expression of affection—*Don't you know that I love you more than life itself?*—began to sound like suicidal threat. Every time I went back to California, I swore on the plane ride back to New York that I would never, ever set foot in the state again. I stopped visiting, stopped calling. I let my sister take up the burden. Since she had been mostly absent for the many years that I lived at home, I told myself it was her turn.

And she was good at it. Over the years Emily had seemingly discovered infinite stores of patience and compassion. After her two years of chopping wood in Idaho, she went on to college and graduated, Phi Beta Kappa, with a degree in women's studies. She moved back to San Francisco, bought a beautiful little house with her girlfriend of many years, and started working for a series of nonprofits—Planned Parenthood, the Bay Area Labor Council. It was as though all of her anger and rebelliousness got shot through the machine of adulthood and came out the other side as political conviction, loyalty, and kindness. I envied her all the more for it. After years of feeling like the dutiful daughter, now I just felt like a complete shit. Clearly I'd missed the window of opportunity to make bad behavior seem glamorous or legendary. When you grow up and act badly, you just let people down.

But no amount of distance or silence could diminish the pull of my mother from the opposite coast, three thousand miles away. I felt it daily as though we were perched on two ends of a long balancing stick. Every night I knew we were each making dinner for ourselves, listening to the radio, starting in on a bottle of wine. I knew we were each thinking of the other, each negotiating our shared store of anxieties and sorrows, each sustained—or hoping to be sustained—by our careers of teaching, reading, and writing.

And now here we were, back in Michigan, walking to and from the courthouse day after day, each toting a legal pad. We take copious notes throughout the trial, as does Solly, Leiterman's wife. My mother and I never speak to Solly, but we hold doors open for one another with a quiet civility, perhaps in tacit acknowledgment of the fact that we can each see that the other's situation here is just a different version of hell. Each morning all three of us send our pads through the court's X-ray machine, where the security guard, who has somehow gotten wind of the fact that I wrote a book about Jane, greets me daily as "the author."

I hadn't written on a legal pad for years. But now I was remembering that I started out writing many years ago on my father's long yellow legal pads. After my parents' divorce, my father occasionally found himself stuck with Emily and me on days when he had to go to work, and he would bring us with him "into the office"—a law firm perched atop a glorious skyscraper in downtown San Francisco. Once up there, to keep me busy, he would give me a legal pad and a pen. That way I could pretend that I, too, was hard at work. My job was to write down everything that happened in the room—my father's hectic pacing, his wild gesticulations on the phone, visits from fellow lawyers, Emily's annoying behavior, the view of the slate-gray harbor below.

After my day of work I would hand my legal pads over to my father for his perusal. He thought they were brilliant. Back in the day when people unthinkingly used their secretaries for terribly inappropriate tasks, he asked his to type them up so they would look more "official"—one long story, told in episodes, entitled *A Day at the Office.*

When I was nine or so this penchant for reportage swerved into an obsession with a tape recorder with which I attempted surreptitiously to record the conversations of my family and friends for about a year. This was before the dawn of the miniature age, the Age of the iPod, and my tape recorder was mammoth, about the size of a portable record player. I had to swaddle it in several blankets or jackets to make it "invisible."

My most successful covert recording from this time captured a conversation during a car ride in which my father was taking me, my best friend Jeanne, Emily, and her best friend China to an ice skating rink. At one point on the tape we pass by a car that has been pulled over by the cops. *The pigs sure are out tonight,* says my father. From the backseat eleven-year-old China warns that you have to be careful with cops. She says she recently heard a story about some cops who came upon a woman being raped, and instead of stopping the rape, they helped.

They helped rape *her,* China clarifies.

Who told you that? Your mother? my father asks.

China's mother was Grace Slick, of the Jefferson Airplane, by this point the Jefferson Starship.

China cackles, then snorts.

I can see it now, on your parents' next album, my father says. "*Snorts by China.*"

China snorts again.

Then I pipe in: *Daddy, why don't women rape men?*

Good question, he muses. *What do you think?*

I don't think women have the passion, I say, with nine-year-old authority.

That's not why, Maggie, Emily says, deeply irritated. *It's not because they don't have the* passion.

MY FATHER wanted me to be a writer. Actually he wanted me to be whatever I wanted to be. Anything I expressed interest in, he would cut out articles about and leave on my pillow for me to discover when I went to bed. In an attempt to make up for the hardship of the divorce, he let Emily and me decorate our rooms at his new house in any way we wanted. I wanted everything in rainbows. I got it. Emily wanted purple everything, purple lamp shades, purple carpet, purple bedspread. She got it, too.

Our life with him in this house was colorful, hedonistic, and brief. Rainbows of light streamed through the stained-glass rainbow that dangled from gold string in front of my bedroom window. I got a pair of rainbow-striped overalls and wore them nearly constantly. He shepherded Stouffer's Macaroni and Beef around on dinner plates and served them to us by candlelight. I performed improvised dance routines for him nightly in his living room, accompanied by loud music from his record collection. Tom Waits. Joni Mitchell. Harry Nilsson. Bob Dylan. He graciously watched these performances from the couch with a lowball of Jack Daniel's in his hand, sometimes nodding off, but always clapping loudly and whistling after my final bow. Other nights he would play the guitar and sing while I climbed onto his back and held on like a monkey. Women came and went, women who would beg along with us, *C'mon, Dad, let's go get ice cream.* At least two were named Candy. There were two Marthas, an Ellen, a Vicki, and two Wendys. At Christmas he bought boxes and boxes of silver tinsel for us to decorate the tree, as tinsel had been forbidden by my mother. Christmas at his house that year was an orgy of tinsel. He would die four weeks later.

For her part, after the divorce my mother had become increasingly taken with the ideal of a minimalist Christmas tree: sparse branches that reached horizontally, decorated solely with white lights, red shellacked apples, and plaid bows. She also took to hanging up a red felt scroll with black-and-white photos of her new husband affixed to it, photos taken when he was a toddler, in the late '50s, sitting on Santa's lap in a tweed overcoat and looking about as petulant as he looked to me now. *Isn't he adorable,* she said each time she passed it. With a kind of measured sadism whose roots continue to elude me, each Christmas my stepfather would wrap up the Chinese Yellow Pages (which my mother couldn't read) and blank VHS tapes (which she had no use for) to give to her as gifts, as if to remind her that he hated the holidays, hated gift-giving, and perhaps on some level hated her (and by extension, us), and that he was committed to performing these hatreds each year with a Dadaesque spirit of invention.

But there was a trick: one year he planted a pair of real pearl earrings at the bottom of this pile of wrapped Wal-Mart garbage, so in subsequent years our mother never knew if a treasure were coming. It never did, but the tension remained high; her disappointment, acute.

After several years of this my mother decided that we should start skipping Christmas altogether and go instead to Mexico, which we then did for a few years in a row. I remember my stepfather being there with us only once. I liked going to Mexico, which generally consisted of climbing steep ruins by day and getting drunk with my mother in beachside bars at night, but the trip always gave me the uneasy feeling that we were on the lam, running from something other than Christmas.

• • •

IN COURT my mother and I quickly discover that sitting on the bench for eight or nine hours at a time is going to be hard on our bodies, so after the first week of the trial we strip the cushions off Jill's porch furniture and start bringing them to court. Solly also starts bringing a cushion. But the cushions only go so far. When I begin to have serious pain down one of my legs and in my shoulder, I tell my mother that I might look into getting a massage somewhere in town.

Go ahead, she says, but personally, she considers massages sybaritic.

I don't know what the word means, so I ignore both it and her.

During the trial I try not to look at what my mother is writing down on her legal pad, but when I do, I notice that we gravitate toward the same details. And I begin to wonder if this is really her story to tell, and if I'm stealing it from her, even now.

Weeks later, back in Connecticut, I look the word up. *Sybarite: a person devoted to pleasure; a voluptuary.* From the Latin *Sybarita,* a native of Sybaris, Italy, whose ancient Greek inhabitants were known for their "notorious luxury."

Apparently my mother also feels it is too sybaritic to sleep with the air conditioner on in her bedroom at Jill's—she says it would be unfair to me, as I do not have one in my little hothouse of a room. The nights are terribly uncomfortable, however, so she ends up making a sort of compromise: each night she turns the air conditioner on, but leaves her windows and door wide open. I try to convince her of the idiocy of this enterprise but she's resolute. During the first week, I get up in the middle of the night, climb out of my twin bed across the hall, and shut her door while she's asleep. I want more privacy, and I suspect she will sleep better if she can at least get cool. But soon I tire of this ritual. After listening to her toss and turn one night, along with the loud, useless hum of the air conditioner, I strip the sheet off my bed, take it downstairs, and start sleeping on the couch.

After Justice

BECAUSE JANE'S boyfriend Phil was the last person to see Jane alive on March 20, 1969, the state has subpoenaed him to appear at the trial. But that's not quite right: the state has asked him to appear, but it did not subpoena him, because you cannot subpoena someone who lives outside the United States. He agrees to come testify, and I find myself feeling a little guilty—I know he doesn't want to, and I was the one who passed information about his whereabouts along to Schroeder back in November. At the time Schroeder joked that I should consider becoming a detective myself, as they'd been looking for Phil for some time with no luck. This perplexed me, as I had found him with one phone call and one overseas letter.

In the time since, Phil and I have met twice for breakfast in Brooklyn, where he keeps an apartment; my mother and I have also flown to see him in London, where we visited for a week with him and his longtime partner, a healthcare activist named Henie. Seeing my mother and Phil greet each other at the London airport after more than thirty years apart made the whole psychotic enterprise of *Jane* seem momentarily worthwhile—restorative, even, albeit in a jagged sort of way.

Phil arrives in Ann Arbor the night before he is to testify, and the state puts him up in the same motel in which my grandfather is staying the night. My mother and I plan to have dinner with Phil alone, partly to catch up, but partly to strategize his encounter with my grandfather. They haven't seen each other since Jane's funeral, and Phil knew then that her father did not approve of him or the relationship. And then there was the icy fact that for some time Phil was also considered a prime suspect in Jane's death, so not only did he suffer the loss of the woman he loved, but he also had to suffer through police interrogations, suspicion from all quarters, searches of his home and car, etc.

When you find the guy, Phil told the police after they were through with him, *I hope you respect his civil rights more than you've respected mine.*

The police could not believe that someone who was planning to marry Jane would speak this way about her killer, so they hauled him back in for more questioning.

Now he bounds out of the motel looking great—an academic version of Richard Gere, wearing black jeans and a black T-shirt. He says he wants to drive by his old house in Ann Arbor, and before long we find ourselves sitting on a brick patio under an umbrella, drinking margaritas, facing the house he used to inhabit, which is now a gay bookstore flanked by this outdoor bar and a Thai restaurant.

For a while Phil stares incredulously at his old house—at the rainbow flag hanging over its door, the customers milling about in its living room—and tells us what it used to look like inside, how it was to be there with Jane. Then his tone suddenly swerves out of the nostalgic and into the interrogatory. He wants to know why my mother and I have committed to attending the whole trial. Why, and for whom, exactly, we think we're there.

We're here for Jane, my mother says plaintively, as if this should be obvious.

I nod in support, even though something about it doesn't ring true. Jane is, after all, quite dead. We're talking about what the living need, or what the living imagine the dead need, or what the living imagine the dead would have wanted were they not dead. But the dead are the dead. Presumably they have finished with wanting.

"To the living we owe respect, / To the dead we owe the truth." ~ *Voltaire.* ~ *Violent Crimes Unit/Michigan State Police,* reads the tagline under each e-mail we receive from Schroeder.

I know I speak for my family in saying we concur with the Voltaire quotation ending your message, my mother writes him back.

It's the state's *case,* Phil now says, with no small portion of disgust. *It doesn't have anything to do with Jane. In fact, she would have hated it.*

My mother and I fidget with the paper umbrellas in our drinks, feeling unexpectedly chastised. He's right: it is not, thankfully, Jane Louise Mixer v. Gary Earl Leiterman. Nor is it Jane Louise Mixer's surviving family v. Gary Earl Leiterman. It is the State of Michigan v. Gary Earl Leiterman. Sitting in court you never forget this fact: you sit squarely facing the judge, who hunkers down in his great black robe in front of a green and white marble wall, an enormous bronze seal of Michigan mounted behind him. The seal consists of an elk and a moose on their hind legs in bas relief, leaning against a crest, which, in turn, depicts a man holding a long gun, beholding a sunrise, underneath the word *TUEBOR*: *I will defend*. Then, wrapped around the bottom of the seal, the state motto: *Si Quaeris Peninsulum Amoenam Circumspice*. *If you seek a pleasant peninsula, look about you*.

But would Jane have hated the trial? She herself was studying to become a lawyer—not a criminal lawyer, but a lawyer nonetheless. *As long as I knew her, she talked about being a lawyer,* her high school teacher told the *Detroit News* a few days after her death. *It was her one ambition*. In 1969 Jane was one of thirty-seven female law students in a class of 420. She spent the last few years of her life working on political campaigns and educating herself about civil rights litigation. In the wake of her death, the law school established the Jane L. Mixer Memorial Award to honor students who demonstrate the most profound commitment to social justice and civil rights. Growing up I always assumed my grandparents set up this award, but I should have known better. In my research for *Jane* I learned that friends of hers set it up in 1970 and have maintained it ever since. Before her case was reopened, initial online searches for "Jane Mixer" mostly conjured up information about former law students who had won this award and later included it on their online CVs. Jane may not have lived long enough to leave behind any "legacy," but if she began one at all, this constellation of political activists, public interest lawyers, and social workers, linked together by her name in cyberspace, might be part of it.

Eventually I break the silence by mumbling something to the effect of, *Maybe Jane would have hated it, but if I were murdered and no one came to the trial, I think I'd feel a little hurt.* The strangeness, the childishness, of this remark is apparent as soon as it leaves my mouth. Of course I wouldn't feel any such thing. I would be dead.

THERE WAS A time in my life, around age sixteen, when I became unsure if women actually died. I mean, I knew that they did, but I became confused as to whether or not they shared in the same existential quandary on the planet that men did. This confusion arose during a summer class I took at UC Berkeley, a lecture course titled "Existentialism in Literature and Film." I had sought out this class for intellectual reasons, but secretly I also hoped it would help me with the panic attacks about death and dying that had beset me in the years immediately following my father's death. His bedroom demise had catapulted the *And if I die before I wake* bedtime prayer from the speculative to the plausible, and though I was but eleven, then twelve, then thirteen, I was often terrified to fall asleep at night lest I would not awaken. For neurological reasons that remain opaque to me, these panic attacks were often accompanied by a certain greenish tint that rinsed my vision. When I felt one coming on I would get out of bed and pace the basement of my mother's house until the furniture and the sky outside and my skin lost this sickly green hue, which, I learned years later on a trip to Kentucky, closely resembles the pall of the air before a tornado.

The professor of Existentialism had told us at the outset that whenever he said "man" he really meant "human." But my brain did not make this substitution easily. I enjoyed the class, but as it went on I felt as though it were an anthropological survey, with this "modern man" as its central object of inquiry—a man whose noirish perambulations and perpetual unease about his mortality were fascinating and familiar to me but nonetheless distinct, and somehow not directly transferable. One of the films we watched in this class was Hitchcock's *Vertigo,* and I remember feeling disconcerted by the way Kim Novak's character seems stranded between ghost and flesh, whereas Jimmy Stewart's seems the "real," incarnate. I wanted to ask my professor afterward whether women were somehow always already dead, or, conversely, had somehow not yet begun to exist, but I could not find a way to formulate this question without sounding, or without feeling, more or less insane.

JANE ASIDE, Phil says, *the state's case strikes me as astonishingly weak.*

My mother and I know a great deal about the state's case, but Phil has a law degree—maybe he knows something we don't?

That may be so, says my mother. *But we're not here because we're hoping "to win." I'm not even sure if we're "after justice." We're here to bear witness.*

I nod again in agreement—and it's a good thing that we're not "after justice," because I doubt if any one of us sitting at this table could articulate exactly what that might mean.

We are only after justice if this person is guilty, my grandfather told the *Kalamazoo Gazette* on November 30, 2004. *I just hope we have the right person and that justice is rendered.*

Perhaps because I have spent hours sermonizing to students about the sins of the passive voice—how it can obfuscate meaning, deaden vitality, and abandon the task of assigning agency or responsibility—I find the grammar of justice maddening. It's always "rendered," "served," or "done." It always swoops down from on high—from God, from the state—like a bolt of lightning, a flaming sword come to separate the righteous from the wicked in Earth's final hour. It is not, apparently, something we can give to one other, something we can make happen, something we can create together down here in the muck. The problem may also lie in the word itself, as for millennia "justice" has meant both "retribution" and "equality," as if a gaping chasm did not separate the two.

If you really want to know what justice is, don't only ask questions and then score off anyone who answers, and refute him, roars Thrasymachus to Socrates in *The Republic. You know very well that it is much easier to ask questions than to answer them. Give an answer yourself and tell us what you say justice is.*

When justice is done, writes Anne Carson, *the world drops away.* This does not seem to me a happy thought. I am not yet sure I want the world to drop away.

Regardless of what happens at the trial, Phil shrugs, as if shaking himself free of the whole mess, *I "processed" this years ago. I dealt with it then, and I moved on. It's over for me now.*

Fair enough, I want to say, but then why are the three of us sitting in front of your old house in Ann Arbor, talking about what Jane would or wouldn't have wanted over margaritas the night before you voluntarily testify at her murder trial? I can't judge the veracity of Phil's pronouncement; I know I shouldn't even try. But I find myself believing it about as much as I believe Sylvia Plath when she writes, *Daddy, daddy, you bastard, I'm through,* in conclusion of a poem utterly sodden with grief and vitriol for her father. Besides, I am beginning to think that there are some events that simply cannot be "processed," some things one never gets "over" or "through."

We drive Phil back to the motel, where we accompany him up to my grandfather's room. They have a perfectly pleasant, if brief, exchange—several notches above civil, a few notches below warm.

Phil's testimony the next morning is stellar. He wears a great suit and is very patient, even with Hiller's final, awful question:

Mr. Weitzman, did you kill Jane Mixer?

No, Phil answers evenly, *I did not.*

I wince, however, when certain photographs of Jane pop up on the big screen—not the autopsy photos, thank

God, but some snapshots that Phil took years ago, which he had kept stored in a safety deposit box before handing them over to me in an envelope in a café in Brooklyn the first time we met, in service of *Jane*. I considered including them in my book but did not. They never felt like mine to reprint—it was more like I'd become their guardian.

But whatever delicacy of intent I may have entertained while writing *Jane* somehow got bungled once Schroeder started calling. Schroeder read the descriptions of these photos in *Jane* and called me right away to ask if I could send him copies of them so that he could have more recent photos to show people during his investigation. I wanted the investigation to go as well as possible—indeed, I felt some sort of ethical imperative to help it go as well as possible—so I quickly made copies of Phil's photos and sent them along. And that is how Phil and I and everyone else came to find ourselves watching them on this large screen, a screen that is being filmed and broadcast live on TV. A guardian of their privacy, indeed.

On the street outside the courthouse, as we wait for a car from the Michigan State Police to bring him back to the airport, Phil tells me he did not sleep well the night before his testimony. He wasn't jet-lagged, nor was he nervous about appearing in court. Rather, he did not sleep well because he had stayed up late in his motel room reading the copy of *Jane* I'd given him at dinner. Before the book went to print I'd asked his permission to use some of our correspondence—permission he had granted, albeit in a diffuse way, by saying that he "trusted me to do the right thing." Nonetheless, now he says he feels quite freaked out by seeing his words in print. (And here I'd been so anxious about the slide show in the courtroom, which he never even mentions, that I'd entirely forgotten to be anxious about his reading *Jane*.) He says that he also noticed that in my "Acknowledgments" I thank him for his friendship. That's nice, he says, but he doesn't really consider what we have a friendship. As he says this I feel my stomach start to curdle, my blood race to my face. *But,* he winks in parting, *that doesn't mean I wouldn't be honored to have one.*

The Book of Shells

On the fourth day of the trial a young forensic scientist named Julie French walks briskly into the courtroom in a blue skirt-suit, raises her right hand and swears to tell the truth, the whole truth, and nothing but the truth (the "so help me God" part is no longer), and unknowingly bursts the all-male bubble. French is but the first of many female forensic scientists to testify, some of whom were not even alive in 1969. The youngest of these women—a peppy DNA analyst in her twenties who looks startlingly young to be deemed an "expert"—estimates that in her work on the World Trade Center attack of Sept. 11, 2001, and the 2004 tsunami in Indonesia, she and her forensic team may have processed hundreds of thousands of individual genetic samples. The 21st century has entered the house.

French's testimony lets loose the flood, and a deluge of complicated DNA testimony follows. We hear so much of it that my mother and I get slaphappy back at Jill's, charting the traces of our bodily fluids throughout the house. We imagine them like invisible Post-it notes, the kind that people put up when they're trying to learn a new language. Sputum from a sneeze on the kitchen faucet. Sweat deposits on our sheets. Blood from used Tampax in the bathroom wastepaper baskets. Tears in our wadded-up balls of Kleenex, and on our sleeves.

In court we learn that some people are "sloughers," meaning that they slough off dead skin cells at a greater rate than others, thus leaving more DNA in their wake. We learn that "sloughing" depends on many things—when you last showered, how much you sweat. We wonder if we are sloughers. We learn that Jane was probably not a big slougher, as very few of her own skin cells show up on her clothing. But Leiterman apparently was, or is, a big slougher.

We learn that Leiterman's DNA was first discovered on Jane's pantyhose in a dark laboratory, by an analyst who laid out each piece of clothing she had been wearing on the night of her murder on a table covered with a sheet of clean brown butcher paper. He then exposed each item to forensic lighting, which "excites biological material." Under UV light certain spots on Jane's pantyhose started to glow, and the analyst bored teeny samples out from these areas and placed them into test tubes. From these samples—each no bigger than a pinprick—he was eventually able to generate a profile, a "DNA fingerprint," that matched that of one man out of 171.7 trillion: Gary Earl Leiterman, of Gobles, Michigan.

We also learn that a third DNA profile was found on Jane's dead body: Phil's. His profile was generated from a mass of cells found on the stomach of her wool jumper, as well as on the paperback copy of Joseph Heller's *Catch-22* that was found beside her dead body. It was Phil's book. He had lent it to her the last time he saw her.

As the stream of analysts testify, I close my eyes and try to imagine what the whole dark laboratory of the world would look like if it were suddenly illuminated by a light, a light whose wavelength "excited" the paths of our bodies through it, and all of our exchanges. If all the blood, shit, cum, sweat, spit, hairs, and tears we have ever shed—onto objects, or onto one another—suddenly started to glow. Phil's skin cells would light up across the belly of Jane's jumper in a streak; Leiterman's would make white pools of light around her ankles, by which she was most likely dragged into the cemetery.

If preserved well these bodily traces can last—and remain identifiable—for decades. For millennia, even, and longer. *DNA is robust,* an analyst explains on the stand. *It can be lost, but it cannot be changed.* Because there is currently no way to date DNA, under the right light, cells from thousands of years ago would glow right alongside the cells we are leaving in our wake today. Under the right light, the present and the past are indistinguishable.

This is bad news for someone hoping to "get away with murder," especially if his or her DNA has somehow made its way into CODIS. I have no plans to murder anyone, but nonetheless I am glad that Schroeder does not ask me to provide a sample of my DNA to the state, as he does my mother, grandfather, and uncle. The state wants genetic profiles related to Jane's on file, so as to eliminate her as a possible contributor to DNA found at the crime scene.

(My grandfather doesn't say it, but I imagine he must be thinking: if this is the alternative to exhuming her body, so be it.) *There's nothing to worry about if you haven't done anything wrong,* advocates of more expansive DNA databases and dragnets say, a refrain Schroeder invokes with a wink as he swabs skin cells from my family's inner cheeks with a fibrous toothbrush, then pulls a special sheath over the samples to protect them until they get to the lab. I can't help remembering that "sheath" bears an etymological relation to "vagina." I'm reminded of this all the more when my mother voices some skepticism about the powers of DNA testing, and Schroeder reassures her, *Look, we had a gang-bang case last weekend, and from the DNA we could even tell which order the guys did her in.*

A SUDDEN DEATH is one way—a terrible way, I suppose—of freezing the details of a life. While writing *Jane* I became amazed by the way that one act of violence had transformed an array of everyday items—a raincoat, a pair of pantyhose, a paperback book, a wool jumper—into numbered pieces of evidence, into talismans that threatened at every turn to take on allegorical proportions. I wanted *Jane* to name these items. I went to great lengths to try to determine whether the raincoat covering Jane's corpse was beige or yellow, for example, as I'd heard both. When I couldn't find out I forced myself to call it "a long raincoat" instead of giving it a color, even though I very much wanted it to have a color. Accuracy felt like a weapon, one means of battling "fate."

Jane had been reading *Catch-22*, but it could have been otherwise. Things can always be otherwise.

During my research I had occasionally come across references to a yellow-and-white striped towel used to catch or wipe up Jane's blood. For reasons that remain unknown to me, detectives have always assumed this towel did not belong to Jane; like the stocking used to strangle her, it is considered an "import into the scene." Some accounts mention it, but others do not. Part of me doubted whether it had ever existed. I included it in *Jane*, but only with a question mark.

For some reason this towel was one of the first things I asked Schroeder about on the phone back in November.

Funny you should mention it, he said. *That towel's sitting right here on my desk.*

The hallway of my apartment took another dive.

So did the courtroom floor, a few months later, as I watched Schroeder snap on latex gloves at the January hearing and pull this towel out of its cardboard evidence box, as if retrieving a piece of flotsam floated in from the far, dark banks of the River Styx. The fabric of reality had to tear a little to allow it into it.

By the time the medical examiner is unfurling this towel at the July trial and describing the nature of the "heavy, intense bloodstain" found in its center, however, the surreal will have given way to the horrible. I may not have known Jane, but I know I share in that blood. So does my mother. So does my sister. I know this every time I see it, and every time I see it I feel like I'm being choked. If asked, I would have described the dense, chaotic, thirty-

six-year-old spiral of dried brown blood as one of the sad-
dest things I've ever seen. *A sorrow beyond dreams.*

The witnesses and detectives fold and unfold this towel
many times, always with a certain solemnity and formality,
as if it were a flag. But the flag of what country, I cannot
say. Some dark crescent of land, a place where suffering is
essentially meaningless, where the present collapses into
the past without warning, where we cannot escape the fates
we fear the most, where heavy rains come and wash bodies up and out of their graves, where grief lasts forever and
its force never fades.

THE TOWEL turns out to be but the overture. One by
one, over the course of the trial, all of the remaining items
from that night make their way out of the evidence box.
Each one comes encased in its own plastic bag, like some
demented load from the dry cleaners. The ritual is as follows: a detective snips each item out of its plastic bag and
hands it to Hiller, who then ceremoniously carries it over
to a medical examiner on the stand, as if passing off a torch.
The examiner then holds each item up for the court and
describes it for the record. During this display I make my
own list:

- one wide, powder-blue scarf, pure silk, very lovely
- one blue-gray jumper, probably wool, tweed-like,
  looks like it hits right above the knee, a silver pin on
  the upper left

- one wool overcoat, you could call it blue or gray (which accounts for the discrepancies of color in newspapers and books), looks bloodstained, hard to tell
- a bunch of clothes on hangers
- one blue turtleneck, looks like cotton, turned inside out, also looks bloody
- one pair of pantyhose, marked all over with little strips of masking tape
- one pale yellow ½ slip bottom, patterned with ladybugs
- one pair of yellow flowered underwear, size 7, also with ladybugs
- one matching bra, more ladybugs
- one crimped, sky-blue headband, about an inch wide, streaked with brown blood.

Whenever the examiner holds up the jumper, the ½ slip, or the coat, the shape of a woman suddenly hangs in the courtroom. Size 7. The shape of Jane. You can see the care she put into the layering, into the coordination of colors: yellows underneath, a scheme of blues on top. Her undergarments might as well have sprung from a time capsule. *Ladybugs,* for God's sake.

Each time "Exhibit 32" appears, a certain hush moves through the room. "Exhibit 32" is the pair of pantyhose Jane was wearing on the night of her murder. The prosecution has also made a digital slide of the hose: a still of two brown legs bent toward each other against a white background. The fate of a man's life depends on this tattered, pigeon-toed pair of pantyhose, whose diaphanous legs now dance emptily in air.

On a different page of my legal pad, I start another list—one that catalogues various words used throughout the trial that agitate me, and why:

- "ligature"—sounds too elegant for a stocking used for garroting
- "debris in the skull"—sounds like garbage, not bullets
- "contusion collar"—sounds like "ring around the collar"
- "wound track"—sounds like a Top 40 song
- "The Book of Shells"—sounds like a children's book about treasures from the sea, not an old ammunition log from a hardware store with Gary's signature in it.

Over the course of the trial smaller, stranger items also straggle out of the box. The oddest of these are not the things that Jane wore or carried, but the things that were taken out of her. The bloody Tampax she had in her vagina on the night of her murder, for example, preserved in a glass jar. Also in glass jars: the two bullets picked out of her brain during her autopsy. One jar is labeled "Brain," the other, "Left temp." The "Left temp" bullet is intact enough to reveal some discernible markings—namely, "six lands and grooves with a right twist." The other, "Brain," is a hopeless pile of lead shards. *Bullets are softer than guns,* a firearms expert for the state explains. *They deform when they hit something hard.* "Brain" entered Jane's head at a very thick spot at the base of her skull, and thus disintegrated immediately.

The jury passes around these little vials of broken lead, squinting at the remains of the shells with bafflement. As they do so the camera from CBS whirls over to my mother and me on our bench, and I can already hear the voice-over: *Family members look on in horror as the jury scrutinizes the debris removed from the victim's skull over thirty years ago.*

But I am not really thinking about this debris. I am thinking about my own box of debris—a little white cardboard box I have carried with me for over twenty-two years, from city to city, apartment to apartment, desk drawer to desk drawer. In this box lie about nine fragments of my father's body, along with some white dust of his bone. My mother, sister, and I scattered his ashes together in a river in the Sierra Nevada back in 1984. But I held on to a handful, which I carried tightly in my fist the whole long drive back down the mountain. I then deposited the remains into this little white box and tied a rubber band around it tightly, intentionally mislabeling it "Dad's high school ring" to throw any thieves off the track. I had big plans for these ashes, plans no one else could know about. Plans no one else had been smart enough to think up. I just didn't know yet what they were. Years later, when I heard the premise of *Jurassic Park*—scientists figure out how to reconstruct dinosaurs from their DNA, and they return to roam the earth—I had the flash: *Perhaps this is what I've been waiting for.*

These ashes are not really ashes, however. They are more like chunks. A few look like I once imagined cremains should look—graceful, moon-colored shards of bone, like seashells chipped and smoothed by the sea. But others are just weird. A spongy, light-beige chunk that could be a miniature rock from Mars. A piece of porous, dark brown matter about as big as an eraser. And, strangest of all, two pieces of porous white bone affixed to what appear to be hunks of dried, bright yellow glue.

I remember asking my mother about these bright yellow hunks shortly after we scattered his ashes. She didn't have an explanation, but she gamely ventured a guess: *Maybe they cremated him while he was still wearing his glasses.*

I found this image bewildering. I contemplated it back at home, alone in my basement room, poking at my little box of ashes, or chunks. I imagined my father being fed into a wood-burning stove like a pizza, his stocky, tan body glimmering in the firelight, entirely naked except for his glasses. I'm still imagining it. The box is sitting right here.

At the Tracks

An ex-boyfriend of mine from long ago has recently moved to Ann Arbor, and one night after court my mother and I go visit him and his family at the quaint house they've just bought in town. His wife's doing a residency in gynecological surgery at the U of M, and they have two kids—a precocious four-year-old named Max, and an adorable baby girl named Tillie. We sit and chat in the kids' playroom, watching Tillie push herself along the carpet on her belly like a seal, and Max masterfully navigate a complicated-looking bridge-building game on the computer. My mother has come along because she got along quite well with this ex-boyfriend, and in fact stayed in touch with him for some time after he and I parted ways. As I listen to them talk and watch her hoist his happy, drooling baby against her hip, I get the sense that I am attending their awkward reunion more than one of my own.

We tell them a little about the trial, and his wife has to remind us repeatedly to spell out words like M-U-R-D-E-R and R-A-P-E so that Max can't understand them. It's hard not to feel as though we are the bearers of seriously bad tidings. *Imports into the scene.* I feel this way all the more as

Max leads me by the hand down to his bedroom to show me some acrobatic tricks on his bed, and I find myself thinking two equally unsettling thoughts: (a) if I had stayed with this boyfriend, maybe this would have been my solid, comprehensible, happy-making life, and (b) Max is about as old as Johnny Ruelas was when he dripped the infamous drop of blood onto the back of Jane's hand.

Once the kids have changed into their pajamas my ex and I decide to peel off to a bar by ourselves to catch up. Not knowing how much he and I will have to say to each other, I tell my mother I'll probably be home early.

At the bar he keeps saying that he can't get over the coincidence of his having just moved here and my being here for a murder trial. Given the many coincidences regarding this case, this one seems slight. I am just glad to see him. We end up drinking quite a bit, and staying out quite late.

To my horror I arrive back at Jill's to find my mother waiting up for me. She was worried. She's upset that I walked home so late alone. I tell her I didn't, that my ex walked me home, there's nothing to worry about, I'm fine, go to sleep. She apologizes, says she thinks the trial is getting to her. Bringing up all her old paranoid fantasies. It doesn't help that she's been reading *The Devil in the White City*, a best seller about a serial rapist/torturer/murderer in Chicago at the turn of the century, which, in an unfortunate stroke of irony, one of the book groups that she leads recently voted their next object of discussion.

Of course my ex didn't walk me home. Instead I wandered, drunk, from Main Street down to the railroad tracks, lay down there and listened to the quiet world. Smoked a cigarette on my back, feeling a part of the ground, one of night's dark and lost creatures.

For as long as I can remember, this has been one of my favorite feelings. To be alone in public, wandering at night, or lying close to the earth, anonymous, invisible, floating. To be "a man of the crowd," or, conversely, alone with Nature or your God. To make your claim on public space even as you feel yourself disappearing into its largesse, into its sublimity. To practice for death by feeling completely empty, but somehow still alive.

It's a sensation that people have tried, in various times and places, to keep women from feeling. Many still try. You've been told a million times that to be alone and female and in public late at night is to court disaster, so it's impossible to know if you're being bold and free or stupid and self-destructive. And sometimes practicing for death is just practicing for death. As a teenager I liked to take baths in the dark with coins placed over my eyes.

As a teenager I also liked to drink. I got drunk for the first time when I was nine, at my mother's wedding reception. Photos from the event show me in a mauve flowered dress, passed out under a glass coffee table, hugging a teddy bear. I had a broken foot at the time, an injury I procured while doing a dance routine for my father, but as everyone thought this injury was a psychosomatic response to my mother's marriage I hadn't yet been to the doctor. In all the photos from the ceremony I am balancing on one foot. I limped down the aisle.

I never told anyone that a few nights before the wedding, alone in my rainbow room at my father's house, I punched my foot repeatedly in an attempt to make the injury visible. It worked, in a way—the ball of my foot swelled up terribly, and the pain got much worse. An X-ray taken a few weeks later revealed stress fractures in a constellation of bones called the "sesamoids," and I came home in yet another cast. I've never known whether I brought on these stress fractures myself, in my bedroom, or whether they stemmed from the initial injury.

But I really learned how to drink, or how not to, when I was fifteen, living in Spain as an exchange student. My entire time there is a blur of *un gintonic, por favor*; Peach Schnapps straight from the bottle in hotel rooms; throwing up whatever late-night *cena* my Spanish host family had served me before I went out to *la discoteca*—I vaguely remember a lot of *tortilla atún*—and then, after throwing up, rinsing out my mouth and going back to the bar; careening around the Spanish countryside in cars driven by drunk strangers; wandering around my midsized, industrial city at night, awed by the then-novel phenomenon of double vision, and by how much better my Spanish was when I was wasted; making out with faceless boy after faceless boy at *la cuadra*, the cluster of bars in my town, in a fog of wet mouths and hard cocks. I learned to appreciate then how being drunk or high siphons off fear, how it facilitates the perilous but deeply relieving feeling of having abandoned, for once and for all, the ongoing project of your safety. Later I will spend about a decade in New York

City working in bars and wandering home near dawn using this same principle.

Lying at the tracks now I mulled over the day's events in court. I thought back to the testimony of a retired state policeman, Earl James, who had spent quite a bit of time discussing the horrific murder of Dawn Basom, the thirteen-year-old girl whose death was number five in the series. James had led the task force on the Michigan Murders back in the '60s, and has since devoted himself to the intrigue of serial murder. (In 1991, he self-published a book titled *Catching Serial Killers* under an imprint he christened "International Forensic Services, Inc.") Perhaps because of this specialization, James tends to speak about Jane's murder with great authority. *She had won awards for debating and it was clear that she had established a rapport with the killer,* he told a reporter during the trial. *But he couldn't let her go because she could identify him.* He would seem to be the only person in the world to have access to such information.

James had tears in his eyes throughout his testimony; Court TV later reported that as he described the rape of Dawn Basom and her subsequent strangulation with electrical wire, "he stared at the ceiling and his voice shook."

James's tears were undoubtedly real, but they did not move me. In fact, they struck me as paternalistic, melodramatic, and more than a little creepy. I simply could not reconcile them with the spectacle of a man engrossed in making animated hand gestures to demonstrate exactly how the killer "sliced through the crotch of Dawn's panties with his knife."

Then I remembered that at some point during his testimony, James had said that Dawn was last seen on the railroad tracks, wandering homeward. And so, lying there, I thought of Dawn. I thought of Dawn, and I thought about how beautiful the railroad tracks are at night, illuminated by red and green signals, the two silver parallel lines gleaming off into the distance. The whole world hushed and hot and flickering.

Gary

As the barest details of what happened to Dawn Basom might indicate, Jane's murder was the least brutal in the series. She appeared to have died quickly, and she was the only one not raped. The prosecution wants to highlight this difference, as it seems to point to a murderer other than Collins. Nancy Grow's son is subpoenaed to say that Jane's bloodstained bag seemed intentionally "propped up" on the side of the road, as though a signpost leading to her body, while a retired cop who worked on the Michigan Murders testifies that the bodies of the other girls were tossed roadside or into ravines like garbage. Whoever killed these girls (Collins, presumably) also revisited them to inflict more damage—the hands and feet of the first victim, a nineteen-year-old named Mary Fleszar, were apparently cut off several days after she died, for example.

The cop who first arrived at Jane's crime scene reemerges to describe how her suitcase and copy of *Catch-22* had been placed close at her side; her shoes, purse, and the yellow-and-white-striped towel between her legs; and her body then elaborately covered—first draped with the clothes on hangers, then with her wool coat, then spread out on top of all that, her raincoat, as if to protect the whole pile from the elements. When asked to compare this treatment to that of Mary Fleszar, this same cop—now an elderly man—just shakes his head. *That first girl, the shape she was in . . .* Hiller has to prod him to continue. *That first girl was just skin and bones. All beaten up with a belt. Her skin,* he says, breaking off, shaking his head again, *her skin was like leather.*

Earl James sums it up on the stand this way: *It almost looked as though the perpetrator of [Jane's] murder showed compassion for the victim.*

The press likes this formulation, and KILLER SHOWED COMPASSION becomes the next day's headline in local and national articles about the case. Court TV builds on the theme, reporting that "the meticulous arrangement of her body showed tenderness."

When Schroeder first questioned Leiterman back in November, he too emphasized these gestures of care. He told Leiterman, *I've worked in homicide a long time, and I've seen things done by absolute monsters. This crime was not committed by a monster. Whoever did this was* not *a monster.* He says this line of talk almost got Leiterman to crack.

I could appreciate this angle as interrogative strategy. But after skimming the KILLER SHOWED COMPASSION headlines at a Starbuck's the next morning before court, my mother and I toss the papers aside in disgust. Shrouding a woman's body as if to protect it from the cold after you've shot her and strangled her and pulled down her underclothes in a final stroke of debasement, carefully arranging the limbs and belongings of a person who will never be able to use either again—together we agree: these acts can-not be classified as "tender."

Schroeder and I had broached this problem months earlier on the phone. I told him then that despite these ges-tures of "care," Jane's vicious post-mortem (or near post-mortem) strangulation hardly seemed to me to indicate remorse or concern for her body.

Well, that's a little complicated, he said.

He told me that upon reexamining the location of the stocking, the nature of its knot, etc., they'd come to sus-pect that it might have been applied as a tourniquet, a somewhat perverse medical effort to stop the bleeding from the gunshot wounds to her head. I couldn't tell whether he meant to suggest that her murderer tied the tourniquet in a fit of guilt or regret, or whether her killer was trying to stop the bleeding for other reasons—not to mess up the upholstery in his car, for example. But I didn't inquire further.

For Schroeder was onto relating another discomfiting speculation. Before entering police work, Schroeder was a Marine. One day early on in the investigation of Jane's case, he was going over some details of the crime scene with another former Marine—particularly how Jane's clothes were piled up, and where her belongings were placed. His friend turned to him and said, *Schroeder, you're the stupidest ex-jarhead I've ever met. Can't you see that this guy was giving her a battlefield burial?*

When a fellow soldier dies in combat and his comrades are unable to remove his body from the field, they are supposed to fold his belongings and place them between his legs so that his corpse and possessions might later be gathered with maximum speed and efficiency. Schroeder was convinced that they were looking for someone who had spent time in the service. Collins had not. Leiterman had.

And for more than twenty years since his time in the service (which took place in South America and Mexico, not Vietnam), Leiterman had been working as a nurse, at Borgess Medical Center.

In that time, it seems more than likely that Leiterman provided many patients with life-sustaining care, perhaps even life-sustaining comfort, along with who knows what else. If he killed Jane, what happens to that care and comfort now? Does it become null and void, retroactively?

At his July trial Leiterman will not resemble the befuddled, scraggly man in a green prison jumpsuit we first saw in January. He will have had a haircut, be wearing a suit and tie, and look much more focused. The shackles binding his ankles will be visible only when the bailiff leads him in and out of the courtroom, at which time he will wave to his family, sometimes cracking a smile.

After this first glimpse of the new Leiterman, however, my mother and I do not see him anymore. To be able to see the big screen, the exhibits shown to the jury, and whomever is testifying, we have to move to a spot on our bench from which he is no longer visible. He will never take the stand, which Hiller tells us is not unusual in capital cases, in which the stakes are so high. We will never hear his voice. Everyone on the witness stand will talk about what "was done" to Jane's body, not what he did or allegedly did, not even what "her murderer did." He will drop out of sight, out of mind, and out of language. It takes a concentrated effort for me to remember him, even now.

I had tried to learn more about Leiterman before the trial, primarily via that lazy, alienating, 21st-century way of learning about anything. I Googled him. Here is what I found:

From the Business section of the Detroit News *on March 23, 2001:*

"I watch the news every evening and night after night for the past year every single financial consultant they interviewed said everything was fine, this was just a little dip," said Gary Leiterman, a registered nurse in Gobles, Mich. In his late 50s, he hoped to switch to a part-time schedule soon. But last year, a week before the market downturn started, his financial planner advised him to move 25% of his assets into aggressive growth funds. Most of that money has since evaporated along with gains on the high-tech Nasdaq market. "When I went back in a couple weeks ago he was a little short with me," Leiterman said. "I'm not going to retire when I'm 60 anymore, that's for sure."

Then, from the "Inside the News" section of the Detroit News *on February 13, 2002:*

Responding to a Jan. 30 Inside the News column on how the newspaper covers women's athletics, reader

Gary Leiterman of Gobles, Mich., maintains there is room for improvement. . . . "The Detroit papers are sadly lacking in their coverage of women's sports. A clear example is the coverage given to the Little League baseball, district, regional, and national tournaments. The same effort is not given to the Little League (girls) Softball World Series Tournament, which is played just two hours away in Kalamazoo. You should be aware that there are over 50,000 women ages 8 to 58 that play fastpitch softball in the state. From strictly a business point of view, if you wanted to increase your readership, this might be a good place to start."

Neither this nurse lamenting his evaporating investments and hoping for early retirement, nor this champion of female athletes everywhere, at home enough as a citizen of the world to write Letters to the Editor, squared easily with the shadowy, fugitive tormentor my mother, sister, and I had been battling for years in my dreams.

Leiterman's reputation as a model citizen was challenged, however, by a headline that appeared about two weeks after his arrest for Jane's murder: SLAYING SUSPECT HIT WITH PORN CHARGE.

When I first got wind of this headline I didn't feel shocked as much as wary, or weary. It seemed too predictable—the next chapter in a classic American story in which the "regular guy" or "good neighbor" turns out to be an ax murderer and/or run a child porn ring out of his basement. In a country in which the porn industry brings in more money than all professional sports combined, I have my doubts as to whether one could search any American home without unearthing a porn stash of one kind or another, much of which would undoubtedly border on illegality. Plus, I like porn, and the only real panic that the words "porn charge" incite in me is that one day my own porn habits might make me a target of the family values revolution when it embarks on the militarized, domestic-invasion leg of its crusade. I called Schroeder right away to get the details.

Schroeder told me that in their search of Leiterman's house after his arrest, the police took into custody two Polaroid pictures, taken with Leiterman's Polaroid camera, which were found in an envelope in a bedside cabinet. The Polaroids depict a young teenage girl, apparently unconscious, naked from the waist down, arranged against the Leitermans' bedspread.

When the police first saw the pictures, they worried they had another homicide on their hands. But when Schroeder saw them, he recognized the girl as the live, sixteen-year-old South Korean exchange student he had met at Leiterman's home on the morning of his arrest.

On December 8, 2004, this exchange student, who spoke very little English, was forced to testify at Leiterman's arraignment on the felony charge of creating sexually abusive material involving a child. She sobbed when shown the pictures, and said she had no memory of their being taken. The police felt fairly sure she had been drugged. In Leiterman's shaving kit, also seized during the search of his home, they later found an unmarked vial of a powdered mixture of diphenhydramine (the active ingredient in Benadryl) and diazepam (that in Valium), which was identified by a state police toxicologist as a knockout potion.

Leiterman maintained that the exchange student was "a wild child," that he did not take the photos of her, but rather came across them. Suspecting they had been taken by one of the girl's boyfriends, he said he was keeping them at his bedside until Solly returned from a business trip so that they could decide together on what action to take next.

Leiterman ultimately pled guilty to the much lesser charge of possession of child pornography, and the girl was sent back to South Korea.

When I hear about this teenage girl sobbing on the stand, it is the first time—and, to be honest, the only time—I feel truly glad that Leiterman has been taken into custody, and remains there.

IN ESSENCE, *the domain of eroticism is the domain of violence, of violation,* wrote the great French pornographic writer Georges Bataille. Bataille was mesmerized by images of Aztecs ripping each other's hearts out of their chests, of Saint Teresa in the throes of a feral ecstasy. I doubt if he had in mind a sweaty old white guy in suburban Michigan churning up powder to knock out and then sexually abuse his exchange student.

• • •

LATER I LEARN that a female coworker once accused Leiterman of sexually molesting her while she was asleep on a bus during a work-sponsored trip. After Leiterman's arrest, a man who lived with him in the late '60s will come forward to tell the police that Leiterman once showed him a vial of liquid and bragged that it would render a woman unconscious, and that too much of it would kill her. The prosecution also unearths a woman Leiterman dated in the late '60s who says she is prepared to testify as to his "sexual dysfunction."

The judge does not allow any of this information to be introduced at the trial. Because Jane was not drugged, he also deems the child porn charge irrelevant. The defense wants to keep it that way, but that means it cannot call any character witnesses to speak on Leiterman's behalf, including Leiterman himself. It will all come down to science.

AT THE START of the trial, I set aside a page in my legal pad to record all the information I will learn about Leiterman over the next few weeks. At the end, this page appeared as follows:

GARY

- nicknames have included "Gus" and "Wimpy"
- known for a healthy appetite
- avid hunter of pheasant, squirrel, deer, rabbit, etc.
- once had a pet fox.

The only other potential insight into Gary's character came in the form of a dirty visual trick used by the prosecution. In a PowerPoint presentation that attempted to match Leiterman's handwriting to the words "Muskegon" and "Mixer" found on the cover of a phone book found by a pay phone in the Law Quad the day after Jane's murder, a handwriting expert for the state took the majority of his samples from letters Gary had written to his family from jail and from the "emotional diary" he was required to keep in drug rehab in 2002.

The first sample appeared on the screen:

The planning started in January when we

Dear Fritzi

The next was more lyrical, albeit truncated:

To me she

I remember Saline clearly from my first

Bring the rain

There's a void in time

He was but one man

Very lonely

The next veered away from this minimalist model, and was a chaotic collage in which the word "ANGRY" recurred about fifty times, often fiercely underlined. Many of the sentences referenced a female object of disaffection, as in *I was so* ANGRY *at her.* Other standout fragments:

If pushed too far . . .

Anger *seething* inside

Leiterman's lawyer immediately objected, saying that the content of the projected material would prejudice the jury. The judge sustained the objection, but allowed the presentation to continue, instructing the jury to perform the perfectly impossible task of ignoring the meaning of the words on the screen and focusing exclusively on their *i*-dots, baselines, pen drags, and initial strokes. But it seemed to me that the jury was riveted by the character being revealed—or constructed—onscreen. So was I. The "Gary" appearing there was pensive and explosive.

While waiting for our egg-and-cheese sandwiches to come off the grill at the court coffeeshop later that day, I chatted with a Michigan State Police detective about the damning subtext of the handwriting presentation. He smiled mischievously. *Yeah, that was pretty low on our part. But given how little information about Gary we've been allowed to bring in, I'm just glad we found a way to convey something of his character.*

I was glad too. But what that "something" was, I cannot say. Was it the fact that Gary carries around a lot of anger? Does that make him more likely to be Jane's murderer? Do the Polaroids of the exchange student? His so-called "sexual dysfunction"? His alleged groping of a fellow nurse on a moving bus? His addiction to painkillers? His pet fox?

Poetic License

THE POET IN me may have loved these little handwriting collages, but the diarist in me was appalled. Having one's intimate musings seized by the police, chopped up into incriminating bits, then projected onto a screen for all to see and later committed to the public record is nothing short of a Kafkaesque nightmare.

It is also one way of describing what I did with Jane's diaries in *Jane*. I had told the CBS producer at dinner that I made use of Jane's journals so that she could speak for herself. That was true. But I also selected the words I wanted, chopped them up, and rearranged them to suit my needs. *Poetic license,* as they say.

Years ago, home alone, about fourteen, I came across a soft, worn leather briefcase in a cabinet in my mother's bedroom. It was a bedside cabinet, about a foot away from my stepfather's jungle machete. I recognized the briefcase at once as my father's. It was full of yellow legal pads, which I pulled out and started reading. Quickly I ascertained that these pads had served as his journals for the last year or so of his life.

The diaries of the dead do not feel inviolable to me, though those of the living do. Perhaps they both should,

I don't know. All I know is that I felt no dread or wrongness in reading these pages. Only curiosity, and sadness.

I learned there that my father had found out about my mother's affair with the housepainter by reading her journal. He had read there that they'd first made love after going on a glider plane ride together, a ride that he had felt suspicious of at the time.

As I read this that day suddenly jumped into focus. I was about seven, maybe eight. We had all gone out for dinner that night to the Peppermill, one of Emily's and my favorite restaurants. Emily and I liked the Peppermill because it had a little pond by the bar with a fire floating miraculously on top, and cocktail waitresses who looked like Charlie's Angels wearing long, salmon-colored evening gowns. Its burgers came with pink plastic spikes in the shape of miniature cows which announced, in tiny red lettering, RARE, MEDIUM, or WELL DONE.

Our parents rarely fought; I rarely even saw them together. But that night there had been a fight, and it had something to do with a glider plane.

I read through his journals once that afternoon and never saw them again. I copped to finding them in a family therapy session—one of a handful of attempts my mother made to keep our new "family unit" from spiraling out of control—and though she and her husband acted understanding in the therapist's office, as soon as we got out I was grounded for snooping. At this same session Emily knocked over the therapist's floor lamp, stormed out of the office, and later had to be discovered then coaxed out from her hiding place between two cars in the underground parking garage before we could go home. The next time I went to look for the briefcase and the legal pads, they were gone.

I remember only a few other fragments.

He referred to me as "the imp," and described me as happy.

He described Emily as quiet and sensitive, and said he was worried about her.

He missed my mother's breasts.

He had recently enjoyed the services of a prostitute on a business trip to Japan, and had especially liked the way that, after each activity, she bestowed a kiss on his penis with a quality he found both delicate and discreet.

Rarely does the man allow himself to be self-indulgent or sexually passive, letting the woman make love to him, my father wrote in an essay called "So You Think You Want to Be a Man?"—an essay that was collected, along with two others, in a little book of his writings his friends put together after his death.

"So You Think You Want to Be a Man?" begins:

For the first 37 years of my life I believed I had been lucky to be a male. After all, men had the best jobs, made the most money, had greater freedom to choose a career, had good women at home as companions and lovers, and generally felt superior to women for these reasons and more. . . . My wife used to say, "Bruce, why are you always so happy? Don't you ever get depressed or angry? You're really missing important feelings; you're missing part of what it is to be an alive human being!" "But Barb," I responded, "I *am* happy. Why should I pretend to have all those feelings I just don't have? What's wrong with being happy 75% of the time?"

A year ago the bottom dropped out. My wife wanted a divorce. She was in love with another man. We separated at her request, and she filed for divorce. What was I to do? Where could I go for help? Feelings new to me were overwhelming: shock, grief and loss dominated my days and nights. I felt helpless. . . . Why was I crying?

He then spends several pages reciting statistics about the various "hazards of being male." Men are 143% more likely to be the victims of aggravated assault, 400% of murder. Women attempt suicide four times more often than men, but men actually succeed in killing themselves three times more often, and so on. But, the eternal optimist, he concludes:

I am not one who has ever enjoyed testimonials, so I will spare you the details. Recall that the introduction to this paper left Bruce Nelson grief-stricken, lonely, and needing help with nowhere to turn. That was a year ago. I reached out to my male friends, and they delivered far beyond my expectations. . . . I realized I had only been half alive for the last several years. The energy created by experiencing the full range has been high indeed.

One night, after taking Emily and me to see the ballet *The Nutcracker,* he unraveled two rolls of toilet paper, wrapped their ends around his hands, and leapt around the living room in a wild impersonation of "The Ribbon Dancer."

He liked to don a rubber Nixon mask without warning and chase Emily and me around his house screaming, *I am not a crook, I am not a crook.*

He sang "Duke of Earl" in a crazy falsetto, and often yelled his personal mantra, *I am immortal until proven not!* at the top of his lungs.

He learned, in the year before he died, how to weep. I saw him.

The End of the Story

AT THE TRIAL I learn that when detectives arrive at the scene of a homicide, they start far away from the body, and move slowly in toward it, so as not to miss or disturb anything, taking photographs, collecting evidence in sweeping, concentric circles.

SEVERAL YEARS ago, while working on *Jane*, I asked my mother if she thought I had grieved my father. I don't know why I thought this was something she could know. But when I think back on the years after his death and try to locate myself in them, I feel like I'm scanning a photograph in which I'm supposed to appear but don't. It occurs to me that in watching me grow up, maybe she saw something I couldn't see.

Shortly after 9/11, some players from the Yankees came down to the fire station next to the bar where I worked in downtown Manhattan. They had come down to sign baseballs for all the kids whose firefighter fathers had died in the World Trade Center towers. Our station, as we called it, lost eleven men, many of whom drank regularly at the bar. I dropped what I was doing and went outside to watch the Yankees play catch with the boys in the street, the air still rank with the stench of the dead and smoldering steel.

The boys were euphoric. None was older than ten or eleven. They shrieked, high-fived, ran after balls in the gutter, and donned the autographed Yankee caps the team members had brought for them. It was impossible to forget that each one had just lost his father. The loss was only a few weeks old; they could not yet know how it would shape the rest of their lives. Watching their little bodies, I wondered where grief gets lodged in such small vessels. If I looked at them long enough, maybe I would actually see it.

The scene was bittersweet, and eventually unbearable. I went back to work.

Of course you grieved, my mother answered me.

FOR YEARS growing up I was secretly furious at our mother for not letting Emily and me into our father's bedroom on the night she found him there, dead. Everyone always said he died in his sleep. But my mother had told us it looked like he'd sat up before falling backwards, so he must have been awake long enough to know that something was going terribly wrong, had just gone terribly wrong, inside his body. Inside his heart. Maybe he woke up with a start, sat up, thinking, *Oh my God, what's happening to me?* Maybe he had fumbled on his bedstand for the telephone, thinking, *I need help.* Or maybe he had fumbled for his glasses, thinking, one last time, *What's happening to me?* If I had seen the traces of this fumbling, I would have been able to tell how long he had suffered. Whether there had been any pain. What his last sound was. His last thought. At the bottom of his staircase, behind the closed door to his bedroom, lay a secret I had been unjustly barred from knowing. If I had been allowed access to it, my dream journals would not have been filled for the next twenty years with imperfect resurrections.

Dad comes back to life, says he had only been in a coma all these years. He explains that after the divorce he got drunk and took a whole mess of anti-depressants and some mystical Mexican drug, that's why he was in the coma. He says some folks at a rehab hospital took him in and never gave up on him, they watched over his body for years waiting for him to twitch. I feel immensely relieved, although a little guilty for giving up on him, and a little angry that it's taken him this long to find us again. Then my mother appears and whispers, don't believe him, nothing he's saying is true, your real father is dead.

Dad, again risen from the dead. He is unbearded and soft and there is something sexual about our relationship. I whisper to him, very close to his face—I'm in graduate school now. He says, Are you going to be a doctor or a lawyer? I say No, Dad, I'm going to be a professor. He smiles and nods. We talk about everything that has happened in his absence. I tell him about the 1989 earthquake; he tells me about an earthquake he remembers in Michigan that happened while he was play-

ing tennis. When he says the court filled with rubble I suspect he's lying. There aren't earthquakes in Michigan. Maybe this is an imposter. Maybe my real father is truly dead, or elsewhere. Then he says he is still immortal, but he has to go now. He has work to do. I think, Oh yes, heaven-type jobs. Heavenly jobs.

My mother was damned any which way. Mostly she was damned because she was alive. If we had found her dead body that night, our loyalty might have swung the other way.

Also, with no other way to explain a massive, fatal heart attack out of the blue at age forty, a story began to circulate like a quiet poison among us that he had died, quite literally, from a broken heart.

She killed him, I overheard Emily tell friends on our school playground, with a shrug.

I too believed this story. But gradually, as the years went by, I awoke to its fallacy. Beyond its medical dubiousness, it also elided the fact that my father had been riding a wave of happiness when he died. He had bloomed, as they say. And after a year or two of seemingly joyous promiscuity, at the time of his death he was considering getting married again. To a woman named Jane.

I had hoped that the years had dissolved this burden for my mother, just as I had hoped that I would eventually stop putting myself in increasingly fucked-up situations in order to make something right that just needed to be left wrong. Then, one afternoon, on a trip home to California during my mother's second divorce, I overheard a wild fight between her and my soon-to-be-ex-stepfather in which he tried to defend his adulterous behavior by reminding her that they, too, had once committed adultery together. From my perch in the guest room I heard her spit back, *You know perfectly well that I paid for that in blood.*

I knew that she was talking about my father, twenty years after the fact. And at that moment I imagined tearing out of the house, running toward the highway, stopping the first car that passed, and begging the driver to take me away, as far away as possible, out of this story.

My mother is a teacher of fiction. She has read every novel under the sun. She wrote her master's thesis at San Francisco State on *Mrs. Dalloway* while pregnant with Emily. To celebrate a poetry publication of mine years ago she sent me a card that read: *"We tell ourselves stories in order to live."—Joan Didion.* At the time I was living in a closet on St. Mark's Place, and I pinned the card to the crumbling wall to remind me of her support, her thoughtfulness.

But the more I looked at the card, the more it troubled me. My poems didn't tell stories. I became a poet in part because I didn't want to tell stories. As far as I could tell, stories may enable us to live, but they also trap us, bring us spectacular pain. In their scramble to make sense of nonsensical things, they distort, codify, blame, aggrandize, restrict, omit, betray, mythologize, you name it. This has always struck me as cause for lament, not celebration. As soon as a writer starts talking about the "human need for narrative" or the "archaic power of storytelling," I usually find myself wanting to bolt out of the auditorium. Otherwise my blood creeps up to my face and begins to boil.

I feel strongly that your family's story of struggle and hope has great relevance to our audience, the young CBS producer wrote. What story was he talking about?

The paradigm of faulty family stories for me has always been that of the demise of my great-uncle Don, who died of MS back in Michigan years ago. Visiting him as a small child terrified me: he lay motionless in his bed after a tracheotomy, and greeted us in husky vibrations mysteriously amplified from a dark hole in his throat. Whenever I asked anyone what had happened to Uncle Don to put this hole in his throat and keep him in bed, I always got the same answer: *It all started one day when Uncle Don stepped on a piece of glass at the beach. He was never the same after that.* It took me years to understand that while this day at the beach might have marked some kind of change in his condition, whatever he stepped on there did not cause his MS. But to this day, the relationship between this piece of sea glass and his eventual neuromuscular meltdown is, in family lore, cement.

During the Middletown winter of murder mind, I was required to teach a course on "narrative theory" at the university. I dismantled the inherited syllabus and made everyone read Beckett, along with an essay about brain damage, then turn in papers focused on the swirling disintegration of storytelling in *Endgame*. Several students seemed to miss the point—assuming there was one—and turned in papers that argued something along the lines of, *If only Hamm and*

Clov could have told coherent, sturdy stories, they might have found lasting happiness. I was brutal on these papers. Several students complained that I seemed unusually hostile to their ideas.

"Nothing is funnier than unhappiness," I repeated back to them, feeling the whirring of some vague, teacherly sadism, clearly in excess of the situation at hand.

I make it real by putting it into words, Virginia Woolf wrote. *It is only by putting it into words that I make it whole; this wholeness means that it has lost its power to hurt me; it gives me, perhaps because by doing so I take away the pain, a great delight to put the severed parts together. Perhaps this is the strongest pleasure known to me.*

How did she end up at the bottom of the River Ouse?

I know what I want is impossible. If I can make my language flat enough, exact enough, if I can rinse each sentence clean enough, like washing a stone over and over again in river water, if I can find the right perch or crevice from which to record everything, if I can give myself enough white space, maybe I could do it. I could tell you this story while walking out of this story. I could—it all could—just disappear.

Photo #5:

Jane's face, in profile, stained by two tracks of dark red blood running from the bullet wound in her left temple. One river of blood runs straight down the side of her cheek; the other emanates from the same source, but runs in a diagonal line across her cheek toward her mouth.

Two brick-red tracks of blood starting to coagulate or already coagulated on Jane's white cheek. That is the picture. That is what there is to see.

But, as the examiner points out, upon scrutiny, this picture tells a story. They all do. This one suggests that Jane was sitting upright when she died, and that the first shot was to her left temple. Gravity would have sent the blood from the first shot running straight down her face. Then, after losing consciousness, her head would have slumped forward onto her chest, changing the course of the flow of blood. Hence the second track, running toward her mouth.

No one knows where Jane died. But from this photo one can imagine that she was sitting upright, in the passenger seat of a car, next to a right-handed killer who shot her first in the left temple, then once again in her lower left skull. I guess to make sure she was dead. And then strangled her. I guess to be very sure.

There are no defense wounds. No signs of a fight. He— Gary, whoever—probably told her not to move. She probably died sitting completely still, the hood of a .22 flat against her left temple, terrified beyond imagining, thinking one simple thought: Please don't kill me.

This is one story the picture tells.

ON APRIL 20, 1970, the poet Paul Celan left his home in Paris, walked to a bridge over the River Seine, and jumped to his death. He left a biography of Hölderlin open on his desk, with the following words underlined: *Some-*

times this genius goes dark and sinks down into the bitter well of his heart.

The sentence does not end there. Celan chose not to underline the rest: *but mostly his apocalyptic star glitters wondrously.*

A FEW YEARS after I received the card from my mother, I sat down to read Didion's 1968–78 essay "The White Album." I knew it opened with the line *We tell ourselves stories in order to live.* I was surprised to discover that by the end of the first paragraph, the essay has already begun to swerve: *Or at least we do for a while.* The pages that follow chronicle a breakdown—Didion's own, and the culture's. The piece closes: *writing has not yet helped me to see what it means.*

I'm sure my mother knew how the essay ended. She chose to give me its beginning.

In the Victim Room

I N 1 9 8 3, the performance artists Linda Montano and Tehching Hsieh tied themselves together with an eight-foot rope around their waists, and lived that way, without touching, for a year.

On the morning of July 22, 2005, I am thinking of Montano and Hsieh while sitting with my family in the "Victim Room" after the jury has gone out to deliberate. A victim's rights advocate named LeAnn has given us a beeper that is supposed to flash and vibrate as soon as the verdict comes in. Once it flashes and vibrates, we have about three minutes to get into the courtroom. The judge will not wait for us—as a courtesy to the defendant, once the jury has reached its verdict, it is to be delivered as swiftly as possible.

So here is the performance piece: everyone in my family who has managed to get themselves to Ann Arbor for the verdict—my grandfather, my mother, my uncle and his wife, my mother's new boyfriend, Emily, and me—must now remain together, huddled around this beeper, not straying any farther than three minutes' distance from the courtroom, for an indefinite period of time, which Hiller tells us could be anywhere from forty minutes to a week.

Beyond the trinity of my mother, Emily, and me, we are not an extraordinarily close family. Before this day no one, including myself, has met my mother's new boyfriend. But now we must all move as one blob, one herd filing into the court coffeeshop together and ordering eight turkey club sandwiches, one herd eating these sandwiches huddled around a table in the Victim Room, which is on the top floor of the courthouse and filled with decks of cards, children's toys, leather couches, and months-old copies of the *New York Times*.

Leiterman's family is offered no Victim Room. Nor do they have a victim's rights advocate named LeAnn, nor a beeper. They have to wait for the verdict sitting, crouching, and sleeping right outside the courtroom, either in the corridor or on a dilapidated U-shaped couch by some vending machines.

I can sense that this performance piece is going to be trying. If it goes on for a week, it might not be sufferable. At first I try to fall asleep on a couch, hoping to shave off some of the initial hours with unconsciousness. When that doesn't work I make an unsuccessful attempt to dismantle an emergency exit a few doors down that looks like it might lead to the roof, thinking I might be able to steal a quick smoke outside. My mother, Emily, and grandfather play hand after hand of gin rummy. My mother's new boyfriend bravely leaves the herd for ten minutes to go buy a current *New York Times* outside in the summer swelter. My uncle sleeps soundly on the couch with the beeper lying against the bare skin of his waist so it will wake him if it trembles.

In the Victim Room

Schroeder pops in the room occasionally, as do the team of detectives we've come to know as PJ, Denise, Bundshuh, and Ken Rochell. There isn't enough room for us all, so they have to hover on the little chairs and stools meant for children, their bulky bodies spilling off the brightly colored plastic. They tell us a little more about their investigation, which, unbeknownst to us, has remained active throughout the trial. Apparently Ruelas has been paging PJ and Bundshuh from prison for days, promising them that he has new information. Ruelas has also been calling Leiterman's attorney with similar promises. The detectives refer to Ruelas as "Satan," and make little devil ears with their hands when they talk about him. *You've never seen someone with blacker eyes*, PJ says, shaking his head. They say it would be unethical to put him on the stand because he's a pathological liar. They're convinced he doesn't know anything, and just wants a chance to escape.

The hours drift on. At the top of the fourth my grandfather asks my mother's new boyfriend what he does for a living. He says, *Picture an imaginary object—a cylinder, for example—and now rotate it in space.* This explanation does not go far. Next he tries to explain by showing us a card trick. He flips over cards from a deck at random, starting a new pile each time he hits a larger number than the card before. He does this several times, and then explains that the equation that dictates how these piles recur is the same as that which determines how fast the lit end of a cigarette will burn.

Her new boyfriend is a theoretical mathematician. He

doesn't crunch numbers—he has a partner who does that for him. His job is to come up with the right questions. As he talks I get the sense that we are in the presence of great genius, and, perhaps, deeper mysteries of the universe than all unsolved murder cases combined.

So how does what you do help the world? my uncle's wife asks cheerily, undoubtedly hoping that the rate at which a cigarette burns might next be tied to the rate at which a tumor metastasizes, or at which the ice caps in the Arctic are currently melting.

It doesn't, he says with a smile, and starts to reshuffle the deck.

At that moment Schroeder's cell phone rings, and we all hear the voice of Denise on the other end: *They're in.*

Our beeper never beeped.

BEYOND MURDER MIND, the worst thing I can imagine is walking to your execution. Movies that contain these scenes upset me more than all other kinds of movie violence combined. After Lars von Trier's *Dancer in the Dark,* which ends with Björk singing and dancing her way to her death on the gallows, I literally could not leave the theater. I thought I might have to be carried out by an usher. This has something to do with my deep-seated opposition to capital punishment, but clearly it goes beyond that. I simply can't bear the idea of walking toward your death knowing you might not be ready for it. Your bowels letting loose, your legs gone to rubber.

Perhaps this is another way of saying that I can't bear the human condition. *Life is like getting into a boat that's just about to sail out to sea and sink,* the Buddhists say. And so it is. Tibetan Buddhists talk about death as a moment of "potent opportunity," but one you have to practice for in order to know what to do with. You have to practice so that even if you were, say, suddenly shot in the head at close range, or even if, say, your heart exploded in your chest in the middle of the night, you'd be instantaneously ready to go, to pass through the bardo. I know that I'm not ready and I'm terrified that I won't learn in time. How can I learn if I'm not even trying?

Of course the worst that can happen, according to the Tibetans, is that you might come back as a hungry ghost or a hell-being and have to take another spin on the wheel of samsara. Sometimes this doesn't sound so bad.

AS WE RUSHED down the courthouse stairs, down the corridor, and into the courtroom, my legs went to rubber. I have no idea why. My life wasn't at stake, nor, at least on the most technical of levels, was Gary's. By the grace of God, Michigan does not have the death penalty. No one in my family had tethered his or her future emotional stability or well-being to a conviction. Thirty-six years is a long time. And while time may feed some families' desire for "justice," it had not done so for mine. None of us really understood the economy in which one life can or should "pay" for another. I'd heard my grandfather say more than once over the past few months that he'd rather have a free Leiterman look him in the eye and admit that he killed his daughter than see him rot in prison claiming his innocence. Over the course of the trial my mother and I had each wondered aloud to one another whether Leiterman should "pay" for Jane's murder (assuming he committed it) by being the best father, grandfather, girls' softball coach, nurse, whatever, that he can be—presuming, of course, that he is no longer a danger to anyone. But Schroeder and Hiller and a host of others think he most definitely is. So might a certain sixteen-year-old girl somewhere back in South Korea.

Perhaps my legs went to rubber for Leiterman's wife, Solly, or for their children, one of whom appeared to be very pregnant. Or for Schroeder, who had so clearly staked his heart and soul on this case, and who now slips me a heart-shaped worrying stone to rub for good luck as the jury files in.

At this point the bailiff—heretofore a pretty jovial guy—suddenly becomes frighteningly serious. He warns us, hand on holster, that if we show any emotion at all when the verdict is read he will immediately eject us from the courthouse. He says that choosing to convict or acquit in a capital case is an extraordinarily difficult decision for a jury to make, and howls of distress from either side will only make their burden harder to bear.

As we sit, the foreman of the jury rises. With little ado, he says they have reached a verdict. He then tells the court that they find the defendant, Gary Earl Leiterman, guilty of murder, first-degree.

The judge thanks them for their service, and they file out of the room. They had deliberated for four and a half hours, including lunch.

As soon as the door shuts behind them my family erupts in a greater outburst of emotion than I ever imagined possible. One look at my grandfather dissolves my entire previous conception of his psychology. This is not the face of a repressed, aloof old man. This is the face of a father now cracking apart with animal sobs. We each take turns holding his frail, ninety-one-year-old body as it crumples under these waves. They aren't waves of relief, just waves of pain, a very old pain that perhaps he himself did not know he housed. Then, for the first time since her death more than twenty years ago, I hear him say my grandmother's name. *Marian should be here,* he sobs.

I try not to look at Leiterman's family. I know they are devastated. "Justice" may have been done, but at this moment the courtroom is simply a room full of broken people, each racked with his or her particular grief, and the air heavy with them all.

THROUGHOUT the trial my mother and I had complained daily about the media presence in the courtroom—about our complete inability to have a "private" moment when at each dramatic, disturbing, or violent turn of events the cameras would pan to our bench, layering our pain with self-consciousness. But back at Jill's the night of the verdict, we all gather around the six o'clock news with an inexplicable, shared hunger to see our experience represented on the screen. We crowd into the living room and flip between the networks for about an hour, waiting for the story to appear. It doesn't. Instead the stations are showcasing two different local stories: that of a three-year-old boy who somehow managed to get up on waterskis on Lake Michigan, and that of the arrest of Aretha Franklin's son, who had attempted to steal a bicycle in a nearby suburb.

The following night my grandfather makes a reservation for us all to have dinner at the Spring Lake Country Club, where he plays golf, a few hours west of Ann Arbor, near Muskegon, where Jane was trying to get to on the last night of her life. Once there we sit around a party table covered with a white tablecloth, next to a plate-glass window overlooking the golf course, which is emptying out due to an oncoming thunderstorm. We all order variations of flounder, the club special. The tone of the dinner is hard to gauge—should we propose a toast? Are we celebrating? How can we celebrate a man's miserable life-to-come in a miserable prison system? In the middle of dinner I excuse myself and pretend to head toward the bathroom but instead veer outside. I wander toward the golf course, which is now humming with the low moo of an alarm signaling the presence of lightning. Where are the Leitermans tonight? What are they eating? Sheets of rain start to sweep the green hills. I fight the urge to lie down on the grass, feel it turn to mud against my face.

A few weeks later, in what would become one of our last conversations, the man I loved told me that while I was away at the trial he had gone swimming in a lake during a lightning storm, and had there had the sudden feeling that perhaps it was our fate to get fatally struck by lightning at the same moment, and thus the whole painful mess we now found ourselves in would evaporate for us both in the same instant. As he said this I pressed the phone close to my ear, as if to imprint his voice against the clay of my brain. And once again I saw this expanse of wet green and mud, and heard the low hum of an alarm.

At the crack of dawn the morning after the country club dinner, I drive my mother, her new boyfriend, and Emily to the airport in Detroit so that they can fly back to California together. I watch their bodies and luggage disappear into the terminal with one slice of the sliding glass doors, pull my car away from the curb, drive around a loop that dumps me back onto the freeway, then speed along mindlessly for some time until I realize that I have no idea where I am and no idea where I'm going. How do I get home from here? Do I head north, through Canada? Do I try to find Ohio? Is Middletown home? My clothes and dishes and books are there, but beyond that I don't really care if I ever go back. My job there is over; my love there is over. When I think of the East Coast all I see is a cavernous darkness, like a museum at night, streaked with fits of bluish-white light, the traces of tears and cum once shed in miscellaneous bedrooms, hotel rooms, parkways, forests, and cars.

I pull over onto the shoulder of the highway and rummage around my station wagon for my torn, outdated road atlas, which, when I find it, might as well be in Cyrillic. My mind does not feel right. Should I go to Niagara Falls? Montreal? What about Akron—didn't my father have a younger brother who once lived in Akron? Where are my father's other siblings, my other aunts and uncles, whom Emily and I have neither seen nor spoken to since his funeral over twenty years ago? Were they even there? Were his parents? I know his mother wasn't—she died the year before my father, at sixty. But was his father? I think he died the following year, also young, but I'm guessing. What did they die of? In my memory my father's father died of grief—the grief of losing his wife, then his most beloved son. Didn't one of my cousins douse himself with gasoline and set himself on fire a few years later? Whatever happened to him? Why couldn't Jane have just driven herself home? Did she simply not have a car of her own? Did women even have cars in 1969?

I lay my head against the steering wheel, feeling the shell of my car shudder with the boom of each car that hurtles past, my map shaking in my lap. *Deadly Ride.* Boom. *This journey of stepping into the light.* Boom. *If I die before I wake.* Boom. *A swift and successful conclusion.* Boom. I begin to weep. There is no place to go.

Primetime

A FEW WEEKS after the trial ends, back on the East Coast, I start repacking my car. Each day I bring a few more things out to it, stuffing vitamins in the glove compartment, tucking a bottle of whiskey in with some blankets in a hamper, shoving pots and pans under the seats, until slowly the apartment becomes empty and the car becomes full.

Oh California, will you take me as I am, strung out on another man, sings Joni Mitchell, in a song I'd been singing my entire life. I started singing this song before I even knew that a world existed outside of California. Then I sang it for fifteen years every time the wheels of the plane from New York City touched down on California soil. Usually I *was* strung out on another man, but in my heart New York was the main man, the one who had made me euphoric and miserable but whom I never really believed I'd have the guts to leave. And now, suddenly, strangely, I was leaving. I'm moving to Los Angeles. It seems as good a place as any other. I don't have a route planned; my plan is simply to point the car west and give myself over to grace. Part of me doubts I'll ever get there, and part of me doesn't care. *California I'm coming home.*

But before I go, I agree to spend my last day in the city doing another interview with *48 Hours Mystery*.

It's hazy and hot, a dog day of summer. I meet up with the crew in an empty loft in Soho kept blissfully dark and cool by black crepe paper stapled over its arched windows. I enjoy the cool air and the free Greek salad they feed me for lunch, but the interview itself is not easy. It goes on for hours, and the correspondent is smart, asking much harder questions than I had anticipated.

At one point she asks me if, while writing *Jane*, I had ever stopped to wonder why murders like the Michigan Murders, or my aunt's murder, occur.

Does she mean serial murder? Torturous murder? Random murder? Rape-and-murder? Just plain-old, run-of-the-mill men killing women?

Of course, I say, flashing on the awful *Sexual Murder: Catathymic and Compulsive Homicides* textbook sitting on my desk like a dirty bomb all winter in the Ponderosa Room. *But it doesn't strike me as the right question.*

She doesn't respond, so I add, *The* why *seems like the obvious part.*

Then she zeros in: *If it's so obvious, then tell us, why do they?*

Remember: QUESTIONS are not evidence, the judge had instructed the jury at the start of the trial. *Only ANSWERS are evidence.*

The answer on the tip of my tongue is a curt one: *Because men hate women.* But I can't say that on national TV without coming off as a rabid, man-hating feminist, nor is it really what I mean. James Ellroy can say it in *My Dark*

Places: *All men hate women for tried-and-true reasons they share in jokes and banter every day. Now you know. You know that half the world will condone what you are just about to do. Look at the bags under the redhead's eyes. Look at her stretch marks. She's putting that cunt rag back in. She's getting blood all over your seat covers—*

Men are animals, my grandfather told me so many times growing up that I began to wonder if he was making some kind of veiled personal confession, or just voicing a lament for his greater tribe.

The most disturbing murderers kill for only one reason—their own enjoyment, declares the voice-over at the start of *Killing for Pleasure,* a History Channel show I chanced upon a few days after the January hearing while channel-surfing at a friend's apartment—a show which featured, to my great surprise, the Michigan Murders. With a grandiosity better suited to an inaugural address, the closing voice-over says that despite their differences, John Collins and the other rapist-murderers featured on the program all share one thing: "the ancient bloodlust of the Greeks and Romans." The parting shot is of the Coliseum.

What can I say? *All men hate women, men are animals?* "*In essence, the domain of eroticism is the domain of violence, of violation*"? "*We live in a society in which there really are fearful and awful people*"? Or, conversely: *Gosh, I have no idea—how could I possibly understand the sick, depraved, monstrous things human beings do to each other, and have apparently done since time immemorial? Might as well chalk it up to* "*the ancient bloodlust of the Greeks and Romans.*" Both answers come out of a script, a script I want out of, a script with two equally lazy endings—cynicism, or incredulity. Neither is right, neither is good enough.

BEFORE WE STARTED this interview, I had vainly asked the correspondent if she thought I should put on some makeup so that I'd look better on camera. I had arrived wearing none, assuming they'd want to cake me up.

She tells me not to worry—they wouldn't be filming me if I didn't look good.

This is primetime, she winks. *No black people, no bad teeth.*

I freeze in horror, then try to go in on the joke.

Not even good-looking white people with bad teeth?

She laughs, shakes her head, adjusts her microphone.

What about good-looking black people with good teeth?

She laughs again, and signals to the camera that we're ready to roll.

Inside I am not laughing. Am I sitting here so that Jane Mixer can join JonBenét Ramsey, Elizabeth Smart, Laci Peterson, Chandra Levy, Natalee Holloway, in the dead-white-girl-of-the-week club? Girls whose lives and deaths, judging by airtime, apparently matter more than all murdered, missing, and suffering brown people combined?

I'm sitting here because I wanted—I still want—Jane's life to "matter." But I don't want it to matter more than others.

Am I sitting here now, months later, in Los Angeles, writing all this down, because I want *my* life to matter? Maybe so. But I don't want it to matter more than others.

I want to remember, or to learn, how to live as if it matters, as if they all matter, even if they don't.

AFTER THE interview the crew asks if I will take them on a little tour of the city, pointing out some places that were important to me while writing *Jane*. At dusk we end up at the main branch of the New York Public Library, where I answer a few more questions on the big marble steps out front. Fifth Avenue is starting to buzz all around us, a languid, soupy summer rush hour. *Yes, this is where I first looked into my aunt's story. Yes, this is where I first embarked on plumbing its deep mystery.*

The narcissistic pleasure is immense. A story that I felt so alone in caring about for so long is suddenly of interest to a camera crew. Years of compulsion, confusion, and damage suddenly gel, right there on the steps, in the light of the camera, in the eyes of intrigued passers-by, into a story. And not just any story—a "story of struggle and hope." I am the hero of this story; perhaps I am even a master warrior.

But standing there on the steps, I feel like a phony. Inside my mind the fragments are rolling loose. The bullet fractured the bone long ago. Now there is but a pile of lead shards, rattling in a glass vial. There is no smoking gun.

NEITHER THE correspondent nor I knew it then, but in just a few weeks Hurricane Katrina would rip in and over the levees of New Orleans, forcing CBS to cancel several weeks of *48 Hours Mystery*, and instead to bring the faces of thousands upon thousands of black people with bad teeth onto primetime—people whose desperation and abandonment by the state made it instantly, abundantly clear exactly how much their lives mattered.

LATE THAT night I return to the trendy hotel in the meatpacking district where CBS has graciously put me up. Not knowing beforehand that the penthouse bar there will be wall-to-wall drunk fashion models, white linen suits, and $18 bright-blue cocktails, I had invited some friends to stop by and say good-bye to me there.

The bar is too loud for conversation, so eventually we give up and crouch on our toadstools, watching the beautiful people do their thing. The most amusing spectacle is a group of Hasidic men getting lap dances from a trio of busty blondes. Things really get going when the blondes tear off the men's yarmulkes and put them on. The Hasidim think this is hilarious, and take several photographs of the half-dressed, yarmulked women with the digital cameras on their cell phones.

Life is a cabaret, toasts one of my friends, gesturing out to the scene. *Come to the cabaret.*

You can also look upon our life as an episode unprofitably disturbing the blessed calm of nothingness, wrote Schopenhauer.

Eventually I take the elevator down to my room, where I lie down to sleep under a wall-sized, framed glass portrait of Kate Moss.

Open Murder

THIS TRIAL HAS done an enormous disservice to both of these families.

So said Leiterman's lawyer at the start of his closing arguments. He went on to say that Leiterman was a father and a grandfather who had been uprooted from his home, where he was needed and loved, incarcerated for months without bail, then forced to stand trial for a decades-old murder he had nothing to do with. Meanwhile my family had been dragged through an agonizing ordeal that had cracked open old wounds, and which would undoubtedly leave us racked with more uncertainty, more pain, and more unanswered questions. At the end of his monologue he approached the jury box and asked theatrically, *Why Jane?* To underscore the fact that there was no apparent motive linking his client to her death, he repeated, *Why Jane? Why Jane?* several more times, as if it were a question no one in my family had ever posed before.

None of it makes any sense, he concluded, shaking his head.

He was right on almost every count.

In his closing arguments, Hiller was as deadpan and meticulous as he had been all along. But to this somber presentation he now added gesture, elaborately miming how the killer would have lifted Jane out of the passenger side of a car and deposited her on the cemetery ground. He was trying to give the jury a visual image of how and why Leiterman's skin cells would have sloughed off around certain parts of her pantyhose, his hands slick with the sweat of adrenaline, the physical expenditure of killing, carrying, and dragging. Throughout this performance it looked as if Hiller were carrying an imaginary bride over the threshold, or putting a ghost to bed.

Having the case reopened 36 years later—is like losing her not once—but twice, my grandfather wrote in his terse, 208-word "victim's impact" statement, addressed "To whom it may concern," which Hiller read aloud at Leiterman's sentencing on August 30, 2005, on which day Leiterman was sentenced to life in prison, without possibility of parole.

I feel no need to—on my part, to offer an apology or any statement of remorse to the Mixer family, Leiterman said on this day, breaking his long silence. *And, as Dr. Mixer mentioned in his letter, to have to live through this trial again last July and hear all that ghastly testimony and view all those ghastly photos. What a horrible feeling. But, I also want to say that I'm innocent of this crime and I'm going to do everything I can within this jurisdictional system to appeal my conviction. And, I guess that's all.*

Someday, when this is all over, I'd love to sit down with you and your family and spin out this whole crazy web, Schroeder had told me at the start. But despite hours of hard work on the part of over a hundred people from various agencies (the Violent Crimes Unit out of Ypsilanti, the Michigan

State Police, the Major Case Team within the Livingston and Washtenaw Narcotics Enforcement Team, and so on), the police and prosecution were eventually unable to discover any links between Leiterman, Ruelas, and Jane. The defense raked the Lansing lab over the coals, but there was never any convincing evidence of lab error or contamination. No one has the faintest idea how the blood of four-year-old "Johnny" got dripped onto the back of Jane's left hand. Leiterman will most likely sit in prison for the rest of his life claiming he never knew Jane, never laid a hand on her, and has no clue how "a mother lode" of his DNA could have gotten all over her pantyhose. As of July 11, 2006, his first appeal has been denied. The whole crazy web will never get spun.

A few weeks after the sentencing, my grandfather finds himself up late watching a "cold case" TV show. The episode has to do with a recent string of murders in Texas. After the show he calls my mother to express concern that maybe this man from Texas actually killed Jane, maybe Leiterman was the wrong guy after all. He says he wants to talk to Schroeder about it; my mother gently discourages him from doing so.

The day after *Deadly Ride* airs in November 2005, I get an e-mail from one of my father's brothers, a man I do not know if I would recognize if he were sitting right here in my living room. *Hopefully, this has given at least some closure to the Mixer family,* he writes. *Wish we had some more closure to Bruce's death. A guess by the doctor as to the cause of death hasn't been much to go on.* A guess by the doctor? I write back immediately and ask if there was some kind of confusion about my father's death that I don't know about. I never hear back.

When I first heard the term "open murder"—the charge upon which Leiterman was originally detained, and which the jury converted to "first-degree"—I did not understand what it meant. I thought I was mishearing the police. But now I know that "open murder" is an intentionally fuzzy charge. It means, essentially, murder without a story.

Even if Leiterman were to "tell all"—assuming he "knows all," whatever that might mean, or that he hasn't eternally repressed whatever it is that he knows—"open murder" would probably remain, for me, the more accurate charge. The incoherence of the act, the suffering it caused—these things are not negotiable.

His lawyer was wrong, however, to term the trial a disservice.

The Hand of God

In March 2005, about halfway between Schroeder's November call and Leiterman's July trial, I decide to go to Michigan to do a reading for *Jane* at a bookstore in Ann Arbor. I fly out to Detroit on a bitterly cold morning, rent a car at the airport, and find a cheap motel nearby to stay the night.

After checking into the motel I find I don't know quite what to do with my day. Michigan feels, as it has always felt to me, claustrophobic and haunted. Though I've only been in the state for two hours I already have the urge to flee. To staple myself into the day I call Schroeder and make a plan to meet him at the Ypsilanti state police post in the afternoon, then to have dinner with him in Ann Arbor before the reading.

I spend the first part of the morning tooling around U of M in my rental car, watching undergraduates swaddled in parkas scurry around the campus. I drive past the impressive, stone Law Quad, where Jane lived at the time of her death, and where my father also once lived. He graduated from the U of M law school in 1968, just a few months before Jane started. I cannot easily imagine him here, but I know his ghost must walk here also.

Then, without really thinking about what I'm doing, I find myself winding out of town on Route 12, the road that leads to Denton Cemetery.

I had been to this spot once before, about three years earlier, while doing research for *Jane.* That visit was part of a painful but momentous trip I took with my mother, during which we traced the path of Jane's final hours to the best of our—or my—knowledge. Going to Denton Cemetery with her then made sense. It felt like a service, to be able to accompany her to a place she'd always wondered about but was too afraid to visit on her own.

Driving down the gray highway now I remember a creepy piece of fiction about the Michigan Murders I'd once found online, a poorly written horror story in which the female narrator and her boyfriend visit all the spots where the dead girls were found. At the last spot they visit together, the boyfriend reveals himself to be the killer, and murders her there. When I read this story I felt sick at the thought of someone visiting all these places to do research for a shoddy piece of writing about a set of murders that had nothing to do with her. Yet here I was, driving my rental car out to the same plot of earth, feeling very much the stranger.

The last time I'd been out this way the cemetery was hard to find. There had been but one small, rusty, easy-to-miss metal sign. This time I'm surprised to find they've "done work" on the place. There are new, clean, and clear signs from the main road. The old chain-link fence, the one that Nancy Grow had been ashamed to pass through, and which my mother and I had once passed through together, has been replaced.

On the gravel road leading to the cemetery entrance I get caught behind a garbage truck making lengthy starts and stops all the way down the street. The two garbagemen look back at me suspiciously for the rest of their ride after I park my car, get out, and stand motionless by the new fence, staring at the muddy ground.

It had been sunny and pastoral, the air buzzing with summer insects, when I was here with my mother. Now it's overcast and freezing, and I feel like a trespasser. A Peeping Tom, with nothing to see.

I couldn't say—I still can't say—what this spot means to me, empty as it is. To me alone, without my mother, without the explanatory shelter of a "family story." I know that Schroeder has also come out here alone on several occasions—to ponder, as a detective, what might have happened to Jane, but also, I suspect, for other reasons, reasons that may remain as unfathomable to him as my own do to me.

One thing feels clear enough, however. The thought of dragging a body out of a car and abandoning it in this frigid, eerie place strikes me as exceptionally cruel. I stay just long enough to have this revelation, then get back in the car and drive to meet Schroeder at his post.

A cop at the desk alerts Schroeder to my arrival over the intercom. He is downstairs in a meeting, and I hear him say playfully, *We're almost done down here, so don't let her out—lock the door behind her.*

As one might imagine, the Violent Crimes Unit at the state police post is the kind of place where you feel locked in just upon entering. For the half hour that I wait there, I listen to the cop at the desk take incoming calls, and chronicle an astonishing litany of abuses. *Yeah, that's an aggravated domestic right there, a felony because he had the gun, then, what? He pistol-whipped her for what? Four hours? Yeah, he'll do some time, he has a history of domestic, and now we'll add another domestic on top of that. OK, sounds good, catch you later.* When I don't feel like listening I wander over to the wall-sized map of the state of Michigan, and mindlessly jot down the finer points of the state's flora and fauna: state bird, ROBIN; state tree, WHITE PINE; state fish, BROOK TROUT; state soil, KALKASKA.

Eventually Schroeder buzzes me in and takes me on a whirlwind tour of the building. Several cops in the hallways ask if I am "the sketch artist"—an identity that has never occurred to me before, but momentarily sounds appealing.

One of the rooms on the tour is Schroeder's office. Above his desk is a strip of photos of the Michigan Murder victims clipped from a '60s newspaper—the same strip I once had pinned over my desk in an attic apartment in Brooklyn, New York, many years ago. To the left of his desk is a high shelf, upon which sit several cardboard evidence boxes. It takes me a moment to realize that these are the evidence boxes from each of the Michigan Murder cases. The girls' last names appear on the side of each box writ large in Magic Marker: FLESZAR. SCHELL. SKELTON. BASOM. KALOM. BEINEMAN.

The Hand of God

I don't know whether to laugh or weep. It feels like the last scene of *Raiders of the Lost Ark,* when the all-important, destructive, and sublime ark has been crated up, and a whistling janitor is wheeling it into an enormous warehouse of identical crates, unwittingly resubmerging its mystery. God only knows what these boxes hold—what "cellular deposits" yet to be decoded, what flakes of dried blood, what ensembles of clothing, what other arbitrary and wrenching mementos from these girls' bodies and lives.

The tour also includes a small room full of dented file cabinets which, Schroeder tells me, he punches whenever he gets angry at all the fucked-up things people do to one another. I can't tell if this is a confession, a performance, or both.

We take separate cars to Ann Arbor and meet up at a dark pub across the street from the bookstore where I'm supposed to read later. We each order hamburgers. Schroeder then tells me that during the span of his investigation of Jane's case, he faced down many demons. He left a bad marriage, quit drinking, fell in love with someone new, and started paying attention to his health, which was seriously in trouble. He takes out his wallet and shows me pictures of his new girlfriend, a social worker named Carol, and her two kids, with whom he says he is having a fantastic time. He especially loves playing with them in the pool.

For the past several years, he tells me, he has been using a photo of Jane as the screen saver on his computer. Most likely it was taken in France, when Jane was there as an exchange student. The picture came from a roll of film that the police found back in 1969 when they searched her room at the Law Quad. Detectives developed the film in the days immediately following her murder, then scoured the prints for clues. The prints yielded none, but eventually provided Schroeder with this glorious photo of Jane. He says he is glad to have a picture of her that differs so dramatically from the crime scene and autopsy photos in her file that he's spent so much time with. He says he showed this photo to Leiterman during his interrogation, in the hopes of eliciting a breakdown. No breakdown occurred, but Schroeder swears that Leiterman appeared shaken.

He says that he doesn't want to spook me, but he wants me to know that on more than one occasion, Jane's ghost has come to him in the middle of the night. He has heard her voice, clearly. He believes that her ghost has come back to transform—even to save—his life, in addition to guiding his investigation. In fact, he believes that all matters related to Jane's case—including my book, and our sitting here together, right now, at this sticky pub table—are being directed by "the hand of God."

I think back to an e-mail Schroeder once sent to my mother, which concluded: *We work for you. Well, actually we always say we work for God (really, just ask me to show you the tattoo on my right arm), but I think you get the point.*

I listen to him and nod with interest as we eat our burgers, all the while feeling a little unnerved. I'm stuck on the image of the ghost of Jane—in her raincoat, her auburn hair held back by her baby-blue headband, her face stained with tracks of blood—whispering to this burly, ruddy-faced cop in the middle of the night. I'm tempted to reinforce my sanity by thinking that whatever voice of Jane's he has heard or hears is whatever he needs to hear to spur him along, personally and professionally. But as he talks I am also remembering times, while working on *Jane*, particularly in the beginning, when I felt a presence with me, especially in my dreams—not something I would call a ghost *per se*, but certainly a presence, something that was very much "me" but also very much "not me."

I'm still not sure, however, who Schroeder's Jane is, or who my Jane is, or what, if anything, they have to do with each other. Whoever or whatever they are, I can't imagine they bear much resemblance to Jane, herself, at all.

Once, after a reading from *Jane*, someone from the audience came up to me and said she thought it was cool that I'd changed my aunt's name to Jane, so that she could become "Jane Doe," plain Jane, an everywoman, a blank screen onto which one could project all one's hopes and fears.

I was interested in what this woman was saying, intellectually, but the idea of taking a person and making her into a blank slate horrified me. It seemed like another form of violence. I hadn't changed Jane's name, but nonetheless I went home wondering if I'd still committed some inchoate but grievous wrong.

Shortly before the trial is set to begin, Schroeder will be hospitalized with a terrible ulcer, which will turn into a stomach-cancer scare. His superiors will take him off Jane's case, citing his health troubles, but also saying that his "powers of objectivity" have come into question. My mother and I will be disappointed, but not surprised. When the trial is over, Schroeder will propose to Carol. They will invite us to the wedding, which will take place on the one-year anniversary of Leiterman's conviction.

But that's all to come. For now Schroeder walks me from the restaurant to my reading, which he had considered attending, but declines after seeing the quiet crowd on folding chairs in the well-lit bookstore. It's just as well. The reading leaves me feeling bizarrely emotional and exposed, as readings can sometimes do. Afterward, as I drive to my dark motel, I feel a familiar species of post-reading loneliness creeping in upon me, amplified by the eeriness of being in the land of Jane's life and death.

I get in bed and turn on the motel TV, hoping to fall asleep as quickly as possible and get out of Michigan first thing in the morning. Instead I find myself wide awake, sucked into a late-night episode of *Law & Order*. The principal story line involves a serial rapist whose trademark is strangulation; the women who have survived his attacks testify in court with reddish-purple rings around their necks, the bruises left over from the rapist's cord.

Photo #6:
No face or body. Just a close-up shot of flesh, white flesh with a dark crease in it. It takes some time to recognize that this is a portrait of a neck, of Jane's neck, after the stocking

was cut out of it. This is the "the furrow is quite deep" photo
Hiller had warned us about. In it Jane's neck appears shaped
like an hourglass, the compressed part in the middle unimag-
inably small, about as wide around as a toilet paper tube
instead of a neck.

This is about as far into the flesh as you can get. If you
squeezed any further, you'd sever it.

When I fall asleep, predictably, promptly, I have a
nightmare. It is a recurring nightmare that starts off, as
many nightmares do, as a beautiful dream. In this dream I
am swimming in a gorgeous, powerful, blue and gold
ocean. My mother is standing back at the shore. The waves
start out small, but quickly grow in size and take me out to
sea. When I look back to the shore, my mother is but a
black dot. Then she is gone. I realize at once that she cannot help me, and that I will die this way.

I know this dream well. Not only because it recurs, but
because it is a restatement of a near-drowning episode from
my childhood. My father had just died, and despite the fact
that we were all in a state of shock, my mother and her husband decided that we should go ahead with a trip to Hawaii
they'd planned months earlier. His six-year-old daughter
from a previous marriage would come with us and spend
the whole trip blotchy and ailing from a mysterious aller-
gic reaction that my mother and her husband insisted on
linking to a pineapple pizza we all shared our first night on
the island.

One day on this excruciating trip we drove out to a

remote black sand beach. Years of swimming in the Pacific had made me feel invincible, uncowed by any riptides Hawaiian waters might throw my way, and I swiftly charged into the water.

After swimming for just a few minutes I looked back at the shore, and found that my new "family unit" appeared as nothing more than specks in the offing. Then, within what felt like seconds, I found myself crashing up against some large, jagged rocks at the far end of the cove. Each enormous wave knocked me down and pinned me there. I couldn't get a breath. Looking down, I noticed that my legs were running with blood.

Despite the chaos of this moment, it felt slow and elongated. And in it I realized, for the first time, that my father was dead. I also realized that my mother could not save me from dying—not now, not ever. I felt a calmness, heard a humming, and had the thought: *So this is how it will end.*

I AWOKE FROM this nightmare into a freezing cold motel room: the heater had broken at some point during the night, and the fan was now blowing icy air into the room.

At first I tried to keep warm under the crappy motel bedspread by thinking about the man I loved. At the time he was traveling in Europe, and was thus unreachable. I didn't know it yet, but as I lay there, he was traveling with another woman. Does it matter now? I tried hard to feel his body wrapped tightly around mine.

The Hand of God

Next I tried to imagine everyone I had ever loved, and everyone who had ever loved me, wrapped around me. I tried to feel that I was the composite of all these people, instead of alone in a shitty motel room with a broken heater somewhere outside of Detroit, a few miles from where Jane's body was dumped thirty-six years ago on a March night just like this one.

Need each other as much as you can bear, writes Eileen Myles. *Everywhere you go in the world.*

I felt the wild need for any or all of these people that night. Lying there alone, I began to feel—perhaps even to know—that I did not exist apart from my love and need of them, nor, perhaps, did they exist apart from their love and need of me.

Of this latter I felt less sure, but it seemed possible, if the equation worked both ways.

Falling asleep I thought, *Maybe this, for me, is the hand of God.*

Coda

A HUGE thunderstorm is rolling into town. My mother and I are sitting on Jill's screened-in porch, sharing a cigarette, as the sky grows dark, the air starting to crack with thunder. The rain, when it comes, comes hard.

Maybe because I grew up in California, I get easily spooked by thunder-and-lightning. It always seems to me a sign that the apocalypse is nigh. But my mother loves big storms. We weather this one in our little mesh box of borrowed porch, as if lowered into the deep sea in a cage to protect us from whatever snub-nosed sharks might come banging at the bars.

We trade some observations about the day's events in court, the orange cherries of our cigarettes bobbing in the darkness, my mother's face intermittently illuminated by purple flashes of lightning. Then gingerly, warily, as if testing out a sore tooth with a darting tongue, we start to talk about the autopsy photos. Maybe talking about them casually on wicker furniture will tame their force. Their anarchy.

I bring up the first shot on the gurney, the one featuring Jane's pale armpit.

She looks so beautiful in that one, my mother says wistfully.

Instantly I want to disagree—partly out of habit, and

193

partly because it sounds as if she's trying to pick out the best of a roll of publicity head shots. But really there's no point in arguing with her. The calm profile of Jane's face, her mouth tipped slightly open, her young skin emanating light—probably a result of the bright flash of the medical examiner's camera, but nonetheless making her skin radiate like the divine in a Renaissance painting—she looks beautiful in that one.

My mother goes on to say that by the time she saw her sister at the funeral home Jane didn't look like herself. She had that strange, bloated, alien look of the several-days dead. But in this photo, taken within hours of her murder, she recognizes her. Even with the dark bullet holes, even with her hair matted with wet and dried blood, even with the stocking buried unutterably deeply in her neck, she recognizes her. She says she is glad to see her again. She says she is glad to see, finally, what was done.

Before we go to sleep, she will open all the windows of Jill's house, so that we can really hear the rain.

I NEVER ENTERED my father's bedroom on the night of his death, but my mother did ask if I wanted to see his body before it was cremated. I said I did. We drove to the funeral home in silence.

She led me into the room where his body was lying on a table, embalmed, wearing one of his business suits. She asked if I wanted a moment alone with him. I said yes, and she left, shutting the door behind her.

Coda

This was the moment I'd been waiting for, the moment that would deliver the solid fact of his absence, the moment that would reveal the secret, the secret that would allow me to let go, to say good-bye.

As soon as she shut the door I felt completely panicked. I scanned the room wildly, like a polar cub on the tundra suddenly separated, potentially fatally, from its pack. I searched the tastefully lit, elegantly furnished room for a place to hide. A red velvet divan seemed a possibility. No one would ever find me. Eventually I would just disappear.

But disappearing was not the task at hand. The task at hand was to approach my father's body, which, sooner or later, I did. He was wearing his glasses, which seemed right but odd, as I knew he did not need them anymore. His hands were folded on his chest and his fingers were dark purple at the tips. He looked like he was trying to keep a straight face, but was about to jump up and call the whole thing off. *I am immortal until proven not!* I looked at him long enough to be sure that this was not the case. Then I told him I loved him, kissed his face, and walked out of the room.

Sources and Resources

Sources

Georges Bataille, *Erotism: Death and Sensuality,* trans. Mary Dalwood (SF: City Lights, 1986)

Samuel Beckett, *Endgame* (NY: Grove Press, 1958)

Anne Carson, *Autobiography of Red* (NY: Vintage, 1998)

Angela Carter, *The Bloody Chamber* (NY: Penguin, 1979)

Pema Chödrön, *The Places That Scare You* (Boston: Shambhala Publications, 2001)

Joan Didion, *The White Album* (NY: Simon & Schuster, 1979)

James Ellroy, *My Dark Places* (NY: Vintage, 1996)

John Felstiner, *Paul Celan: Poet, Survivor, Jew* (New Haven: Yale University Press, 1995)

Edward Keyes, *The Michigan Murders* (NY: Pocket Books, 1976)

Thomas Merton, *No Man Is an Island* (San Diego: Harcourt Brace & Co., 1955)

Joni Mitchell, "California," from *Blue* (Reprise Records, 1971)

Michael S. Moore, "A Defense of the Retributivist View," in *What Is Justice?*, ed. Robert C. Solomon and Mark C. Murphy (NY, Oxford: Oxford University Press, 2000)

Eileen Myles, "To the Class of '92," in *Maxfield Parrish: New and Selected Poems* (Santa Rosa, CA: Black Sparrow, 1995)

Sources and Resources

Bruce Nelson, *Papers* (printed by Charles M. Hobson III, 1984)

Adam Phillips, *Winnicott* (Cambridge: Harvard University Press, 1988)

Plato, *The Republic and Other Works,* trans. B. Jowett (NY: Anchor Books, 1989)

Arthur Schopenhauer, *Essays and Aphorisms,* trans. R. J. Hollingdale (NY: Penguin, 1970)

Paul Schrader, screenplay for *Taxi Driver* (1976)

Virginia Woolf, *Moments of Being,* ed. Jeanne Schulkind (San Diego: Harcourt Brace & Co., 1985)

Resources

American Civil Liberties Union, www.aclu.org

Citizens United for Alternatives to the Death Penalty, www.cuadp.org

Combined DNA Index System, www.fbi.gov/hq/lab/codis

Critical Resistance, www.criticalresistance.org

Death Penalty Information Center, www.deathpenaltyinfo.org

DNA Fingerprinting and Civil Liberties Project of the American Society of Law, Medicine, & Ethics, www.aslme.org/dna_04

Fairness and Accuracy in Reporting, www.fair.org

INCITE!, Women of Color Against Violence, www.incite-national.org

The Innocence Project, www.innocenceproject.org

The Justice Project, www.justiceproject.org

Murder Victims' Families for Human Rights, www.willsworld.com/~mvfhr

Murder Victims' Families for Reconciliation, www.mvfr.org

360 Degrees: Perspectives on the U.S. Criminal Justice System, www.360degrees.org

Acknowledgments

Thank you PJ Mark, Liz Stein, Maris Kreizman, Amra Brooks, Brian Blanchfield, Matthew Sharpe, Suzanne Snider, Wayne Koestenbaum, Janet Sarbanes, Mady Schutzman, Eileen Myles, Sally Baumer, Lauren Sanders, Richard Nash, Cort Day, Kate Egan, Jordana Rosenberg, Lily Mazzarella, Gretchen Hildebran, Judy Kann, the Michigan State Police—especially Detective-Sergeants Eric Schroeder, Denise Powell, Patrick "PJ" Moore, James Bundshuh, and Kenneth Rochell—Deputy Chief Assistant Prosecutor Steven Hiller, Victim/Witness Advocate LeAnn Kaiser, Maureen Maher, Chris Young, and Gail Zimmerman of CBS News, Dan and Lynne Mixer, Dr. Dan Mixer, Jill Johnson, Kristi Gilbert, Phil Weitzman, Craig Tracy, Kat Hartman, Barbara Nelson, and Emily Jane Nelson. This book would not have been possible without their intelligence, generosity, and humanity.